CHAIRING
— AN —
ACADEMIC
DEPARTMENT

Walter H. Gmelch
Val D. Miskin

Atwood Publishing
Madison, Wisconsin

Chairing an Academic Department
By Walter H. Gmelch and Val D. Miskin
ISBN: 1-891859-52-8

© 2004, Atwood Publishing, Madison, Wisconsin
www.atwoodpublishing.com

Cover design by Tamara Dever, TLC Graphics, www.tlcgraphics.com

Library of Congress Cataloging-in-Publication Data

Gmelch, Walter H.
  Chairing an academic department / Walter H. Gmelch, Val D. Miskin.— 2nd ed.
     p. cm.
  Includes bibliographical references (p.) and index.
  ISBN 1-891859-52-8 (pbk.)
  1. Departmental chairmen (Universities)—United States. I. Miskin, Val D., 1944-
II. Title.

  LB2341.G555 2004
  378.1'11'0973—dc22
                            2004006859

To my loving parents,
the heart, mind and soul of my life and profession:

Edna B. Gmelch: 1922-2003
George J. Gmelch: 1919-2003

TABLE OF CONTENTS

— Introduction —

THE CALL TO LEADERSHIP

Around the world, scholars and administrators alike speak about a great leadership crisis in higher education. Blue ribbon commissions and executive reports from the American Council on Education (Eckel, Green, and Hill 2001), the Kellogg Commission (Astin and Astin 2000), and the Kellogg Foundation (Beineke and Sublett 1999) to the Global Consortium of Higher Education (Acker 1999; Gmelch 2001) call for bolder and better college and university leadership. Innovations and transformation of universities will not become a reality unless we build the leadership capacity. The search for solutions to the leadership dilemma leads us to thousands of leadership studies, most of which are contradictory and inconclusive. Leaders: are born, not made—made, not born; possess distinctive traits—possess no special traits at all; emerge from the ranks of faculty—must be trained and developed; must use power and influence—merely manage symbols and the academic culture.

While the corporate world complains that they have simply progressed from the Bronze Age of leadership to the Iron Age, we fear that higher education may still be in the Dark Ages. We hope that this book will shed some light that will lead all of us into the Building Age of department chairs.

Rarely do we study or even discuss the questions that impede our ability to attract and prepare academic leaders. Institutional searches for academic leaders are failing more often now than in the past. Many of these searches are going into their second, third, or even fourth cycles. When positions go unfilled, bad things happen—institutions suffer from lack of leadership, departments suffer from lack of representation, faculty suffer from lack of a strong voice of advocacy, states suffer from lack of connection and communication, and the profession suffers from the void that is at best temporarily created (Andersen 2002).

Historically, academic leaders appear to have undergone a transformation from chief academic officer to chief executive officer, with more emphasis placed on extramural funding, personnel decision making, and alumni relations. Increasingly, the vision of an academic leader (e.g., lead faculty member, department chair, dean, provost, rector, or president) as a quiet, scholarly leader has been overtaken by the executive image of one who is politically astute and economically savvy. Some view the role of academic leader as a *dove* of peace intervening among warring factions that are causing destructive turbulence in the college, a *dragon* driving away internal or external forces that threaten the department, and a *diplomat* guiding, inspiring, and encouraging people who live and work in the department (Tucker and Bryan 1988). No matter what the view, today's leader in the academy resembles a species with an imperiled existence.

What is going on? Some conclude that colleges are almost impossible to manage well and that academics who are trying to run or repair them are getting burned out and eased out with astonishing speed. It is a terribly difficult balancing act.

THE ACADEMIC LEADERSHIP CHALLENGE

Academic leaders typically come to their positions without leadership training; without prior executive experience; without a clear understanding of the ambiguity and complexity of their roles; without recognition of the metamorphic changes that occur as one transforms from an academic to an academic leader; and without an awareness of the cost to their academic and personal lives (Gmelch 2004). The search for solutions to this leadership void leads us to realize that the academic leader may be the least studied and most misunderstood management position anywhere in the world. The transformation to academic leadership takes time and dedication, and not all faculty make the complete transition to leadership.

The Call without Leadership Training

To become an expert takes time. Studies of experts in the corporate world who attain international levels of performance point to the 10-year rule of preparation (Ericsson, Krampe, and Tesch-Romer 1993; Ericsson and Smith 1991). In the American university, seven years represents the threshold for faculty to attain the status of expert in order to achieve tenure and promotion at the associate professor level, and another seven years for full membership in the academy. If it takes 7 to 14 years to achieve expertise in our academic disciplines, why do we assume we can create an academic leader with a weekend seminar? Does the Ph.D. represent a terminal degree, almost like a terminal illness? Few universities and colleges have systematic training for their academic leaders and of the more than 2,000 academic leaders we have surveyed, only 3 percent have department chair development programs in their universities. As we all may now appreciate, we need a radical change in our approach to leadership development in higher education.

The Call without Administrative Experience

The time of amateur administration is over. Department chairs often see themselves as scholars who, out of a sense of duty, temporarily accept responsibility for administrative tasks so other professors can continue with their teaching and scholarly pursuits. Nearly 50,000 scholars in the United State currently serve as department chairs, and almost one-quarter will need to be replaced each year. Department chairs and deans serve six years on the average, and university presidents four years (Gmelch, Burns, et al. 1992; Gmelch, Sarros, et al. 1998). We have already established that opportunities for individual skill development through training is woefully inadequate, but what are we doing to provide leadership experiences to prepare our next generation of academic leaders? Even if we had systematic skill development opportunities available, if you asked managers where they learned their leadership abilities, most will tell you from their job experiences. In fact, a poll of 1,450 managers from 12 corporations cited experience, not the classroom, as the best teacher for leadership (Ready 1994). One should not draw the conclusion that formal training and education are of limited value; academic leadership training, in combination with experience and socialization, can heighten faculty members' appreciation for leadership and strengthen their motivation to develop leadership capabilities.

The Call without Understanding Role Conflict and Ambiguity

Caught between conflicting interests of faculty and administration, trying to look in two directions—department chairs often don't know which way to turn. They mediate the concerns of the university mission to faculty, and at the same time, they try to champion the values of their faculty. As a result, they find themselves swiveling between their faculty colleagues and university administration. In essence, they are caught in the godlike role of Janus, a Roman god with two faces looking in two directions at the same time. While academic leaders don't have to worry about being deified, they find themselves in a unique position—a leadership role that has no parallel in business or industry (Gmelch and Miskin 1993). To balance their roles, they must learn to swivel without appearing dizzy, schizophrenic, or "two-faced." They must employ a facilitative leadership style while working with faculty in the academic core and a more traditional line-authoritative style with the administrative core.

The Call without Recognition of Metamorphic Changes

Faculty spend, on the average, 16 years in their discipline before venturing into academic leadership (Carroll and Wolverton 2004). After all these years of socialization, how do faculty make the transition into academic leadership? A national study of beginning department chairs in the United States identified salient patterns that characterize the "metamorphosis" from faculty-centered to leader-centered. There has been a shift from:

1. solitary to social—faculty typically work alone on research, preparing for teaching and other projects, while leaders must learn to work with others;

2. focused to fragmented—faculty have long, uninterrupted periods for scholarly pursuits, while the leader's position is characterized by brevity, variety, and fragmentation;

3. autonomy to accountability—faculty enjoy autonomy, while leaders become accountable to faculty in the department and to central administration;

4. manuscripts to memoranda—faculty carefully critique and review their manuscripts, while leaders must learn the art of writing succinct, clear memos in a short amount of time;

5. private to public—faculty may block out long periods of time for scholarly work, while leaders have an obligation to be accessible throughout the day to the many constituencies they serve;

6. professing to persuading—acting in the role of expert, faculty disseminate information, while leaders profess less and build consensus more;

7. stability to mobility—faculty inquire and grow professionally within the stability of their discipline and circle of professional acquaintances, while leaders must be more mobile, visible, and political;

8. client to custodian—faculty act as clients, requesting and expecting university resources, while the leader is a custodian and dispenser of resources; and

9. austerity to prosperity—while the difference in salary between faculty and administrator may be insignificant, the new experience of having control over resources may lead the academic leader to develop an illusion of considerable "prosperity" (Gmelch and Seedorf 1989; Gmelch and Parkay 1999).

Figure I.1. The Transformation from Professor to Chair

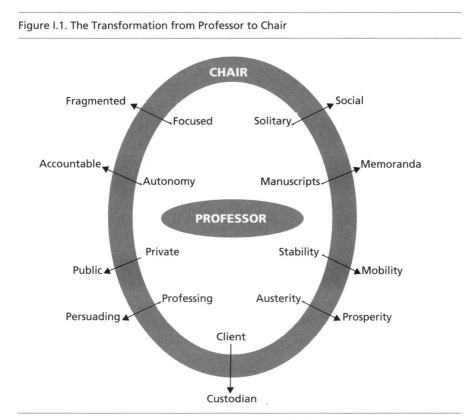

SOURCE: Reprinted with permission from *Leadership Skills for Department Chairs* by Walter H. Gmelch and Val D. Miskin, 1993, p. 16.

The metamorphosis from professor to academic leader takes time and dedication (see Figure I.1). Not all make the complete transition, and in fact, few department chairs become fully socialized into leadership.

The Call without an Awareness of the Cost to Scholarship

Academic leaders try to retain their identity as scholars while serving in administration. Not surprisingly, with 16 years of socialization in their discipline before entering administration, most academic leaders feel most comfortable and competent in their scholar role. In fact, 65 percent of department chairs return to faculty status after serving in their administrative capacity and therefore are wise to protect their scholarly interests. They express frustration at their inability to spend much time pursuing academic agendas. "Having insufficient time to remain current in my discipline" causes the greatest stress for department chairs and ranks third for deans (Gmelch and Burns 1994). Most department chairs would spend more time on their own academic endeavors if they could but find it virtually impossible because of the demands of leadership duties. If we are to build a sustained leadership capacity within our universities, we must address the issue of balance in the academic leader's life.

The Search for Department Chairs

In today's world, many of us dream of balance and serenity—if not in our professions, at least in our personal lives. Department chairs are no exception. For many, work becomes their entire life. One of the prices they pay when they accept a leadership position is an incredible time commitment —and the pressure to find balance in their lives. Their role brings with it an identity and self-concept that often dictates who they socialize with, where they live, how long they retain their position, and what lifestyle they lead. Obviously, being in a leadership capacity is an important part of their lives and provides them with pleasures as well as pressures.

Pressures over the past two decades have begun to transform the once unquestioning academic administrator into an individual struggling to find balance between total academic immersion and a fulfilled private life. Psychologists suggest that one cannot be unhealthy or ineffective in private life and still be an effective professional.

Finally, experts contend that the state of selection of the top three levels of the organization is precarious at best (Sessa and Taylor 2000)— including presidents, provosts, and deans, although one might even question the state of selecting department chairs. Why? First, universities and colleges have very little expertise in the selection of executives and at times leave that process to executive search firms. Also, executives themselves do not feel particularly competent in the skills needed in selection and therefore gravitate to the more pressing day-to-day needs. Finally, most institutions of higher education have inadequate hiring, training, promotion, and succession-planning systems.

Building the Leadership Capacity: An Agenda for Action

We conclude this introduction with the realization that leadership talent on the global scene is scarce. The need for effective leadership to transform universities has never been greater. As a result, we hope to turn the discussion to ways we all can develop an agenda to build leadership capacity within institutions of higher education.

From the corporate sector, we find that there are three principal approaches to leadership education: individual skill development, socializa-

---

Figure I.2. Department Chair Development

Conceptual Understanding

Skill Development

Reflective Practice

---

tion of leaders values and visions, and strategic interventions that promote collective vision (Conger and Benjamin 1999). In higher education, leadership development is at a critical juncture. We need to prepare department chairs with the conceptual understanding of how universities work (Birnbaum 1990), equip them with the skills to meet the leadership challenges (Higgerson 1996; Lucas 2000; Thomas and Schuh 2004; Wolverton and Gmelch 2002), and build reflection into their practice (Schon 1983) as they go down the path of leadership (see Figure I.2). Again, while the corporate world complains that they have simply progressed from the Bronze Age of leadership to the Iron Age, it is our hope that this book will help lead us into the Enlightenment Age of academic leadership.

Chapter 1

Department Chair Roles

— Weaving the Web —

> A good executive is multifaceted like a diamond.
> The larger the number of facets,
> the more brilliantly it shines.
> —Henry Levinson

This Book and You

This book is about what it takes to be an effective department chair. Chairs lead complex lives, but they worry most about and work hardest at managing, leading, developing faculty, and maintaining their scholarship. Mastery of any one of these four roles is difficult at best; mastery of all of them is miraculous. Only eight of the several hundred chairs we have studied claimed to perform exceptionally well in all four roles. Nevertheless, success at any one of the four activities rarely comes in isolation from the other three.

Our discussion in this book is based on the four roles of faculty developer, manager, leader, and scholar, as discovered in our survey of hundreds of chairs and now applied to the craft of being a department chair. Keep these in mind as you are hired for, trained in, and socialized into your position. Your challenge is to weave all four roles together into a rewarding position within a productive department.

Your Move to Department Chair

Congratulations! If you have picked up this book, you either must want to be or currently are serving as the chair of your department. After

Table 1.1. Why Faculty Become Department Chairs

REASON FOR SERVING	NUMBER OF CHAIRS
1. For personal development (interesting, challenge, new opportunities)	321
2. Drafted by the dean or my colleagues	251
3. Out of necessity (lack of alternative candidates)	196
4. To be more in control of my environment	161
5. Out of sense of duty, it was my turn	133
6. For financial gain	117
7. An opportunity to relocate at new institution	101

SOURCE: Reprinted with permission from *Leadership Skills for Department Chairs,* by Walter H. Gmelch and Val D. Miskin, p. 6, 1993, Anker Publishing Company, Inc.

years of dedication to the academic side of the enterprise—teaching, performing, researching, writing, and serving on committees in the academy—finally you have been recognized for your outstanding contributions and have been elevated to serving your institution and your colleagues as a department chair. Or is that really the way it happens?

Maybe it is time to hear the rest of the story. A slightly different scenario is depicted by the results of four national studies, using both interviews and surveys, conducted by the Center for the Study of the Department Chair (now the Center for the Study of Academic Leadership) (Gmelch, Burns, et al. 1992; Gmelch, Carroll, et al. 1990; Houchen and Gmelch, 1994; Gmelch, Wolverton, et al. 1996) and two international studies of heads of departments and deans (Gmelch and Sarros 1996; Gmelch, Sarros, et al. 1998). Why do professors choose to serve as department chairs? Table 1.1 lists some of the most common reasons. First and foremost, they do it for reasons of personal development: searching for new opportunities, seeking an interesting challenge, being more in control of their environment, and other intrinsically satisfying motives. Second, many chairs have been confronted with "an offer they couldn't refuse." Literally, they have been drafted by the dean or their colleagues. If the external pressure of being drafted by the dean were not enough, other chairs said they had no other choice—they were "scared to death of the alternative."

One of the anonymous reviewers who read this book in manuscript confirmed our research in humorous, David Letterman style, with this list of the "Top 10 Reasons Professors Become Chairs":

10. Because you don't want someone else to do it even if you don't.

9. Because you are burned out teaching the same thing over and over again for 20 years and writing articles two people in the whole country read.

8. For the money.

7. For the petty power, having, in middle age, experienced a precipitous decline . . . and needing an alternative thrill.

6. Because you lack imagination and can't think of anything better and more original to do.

5. Because you have imagination and fantasize about all the things you will do back to your peers that they did to you while they were chair.

4. Because some dean has made you an offer you can't refuse.

3. Because your peers elect you to slow down your rate-busting activity by loading you up with administrative trivia.

2. Because your peers elect you, thinking you are useless at research and teaching and this way you can at least fill out administrative reports.

1. Because you temporarily became insane, forgetting why you came into academics in the first place, momentarily in a state of confusion, mistaking your little college or university for General Motors or Microsoft, thinking you will climb the ladder.

Think about what motivated you to serve as department chair. Does it make a difference? You bet it does. Of those who are serving because of the expected intrinsic rewards, we can expect about two-thirds to become committed to this leadership position and to serve another term. Of those who were forced into the position by external pressures, however, only a third will return; the rest of you will just take your turn for a term (Gmelch, Carroll, et al. 1990). As you can see, this creates a leadership crisis in the most critical leadership position in higher education. After all, it is at the department level where the customers are educated and completed as graduates. The time has come to end "amateur administration." Your sense of duty must be combined with a strong commitment to the position and its challenges and responsibilities.

But, you say, you are not sure of the new roles chairs have to play, and you have not been trained to take over such a weighty responsibility. You are not alone. Most chairs come to their positions without leadership training, without prior administrative experience, and without a clear understanding of their role. Being promoted to department chair is akin to white-water rafting without a life jacket and not knowing how to swim. If you are in up to your neck, consider this book a lifeline.

Your successful transition from professor to department chair begins with learning new ways of thinking and perceiving your roles. Your point of reference, the way you were academically socialized for more than a decade as a faculty member, will be challenged dramatically. You will move from the inner-oriented faculty psyche of being focused, autonomous, private, solitary, and a client of the department to the outer-oriented psyche of being fragmented, accountable, public, social, and custodian of the department (Gmelch and Seedorf 1989). To perform your new job, you will need to weave a new web of roles into the scholarly robe you already wear.

THE WEB WE WEAVE

Chairs keep busy. Endless meetings, stacks of paperwork, constant interruptions, and fragmented encounters on a multitude of topics set the pace of a sprinter running long distances. But what is most important to you and your faculty? All the memos, meetings, phone calls, budgets, drop-in visitors, and confrontations represent means, but do these activities produce the desired results for the department?

Do department chairs have influence over, or pay attention to, the most important activities? If so, what are they? With so much to do, how do they choose what to do first? Virtually every book on management lists and exalts the tasks, duties, roles, and responsibilities of administrators. Lists specific to department chair duties range widely, from the exhaustive listing of 97 activities discovered by a University of Nebraska research team (Creswell, Wheeler, et al. 1990) to the 54 varieties of tasks and duties cited in Allen Tucker's classic book *Chairing the Academic Department* (1992) to the 40 functions forwarded in a study of Australian department chairs (Moses and Roe 1990) to the lists of chair duties studied and categorized by scholars (Gmelch and Miskin 1993; Seagren, Creswell, and Wheeler 1993; Smart and Elton 1976).

Typical faculty manuals at most colleges and universities provide lists of chairs' duties and responsibilities, such as organizing and supervising curriculum, distributing teaching research loads, supervising department funds, and recommending promotions and salaries. Check your college manual for your own local specifications. Note, however, that although the numerous lists available appear refined and comprehensive, they actually represent fragmented activities.

The functional needs of faculty and the behavioral requirements of department chairs help determine the roles played by chairs in higher education. The things that faculty members and chairs expect of each other result in a diverse set of roles for department chairs. We began our research for this book by asking 800 department chairs from colleges and universities across the United States to identify their most important tasks. From statistical analysis of these lists emerged four comprehensive roles of the chair that are critical to department productivity and faculty survival: faculty developer, manager, leader, and scholar (Carroll and Gmelch 1992; Gmelch and Miskin 1993). These four roles form the basis of our discussion in this book.

FOUR CHAIR ROLES

Remember the management axiom: What you pay attention to is what employees believe is important. Ask yourself where your energies are currently being expended in your position as department chair. Department chairs' 12 most important tasks are listed in Table 1.2 (Gmelch, Burns, et al. 1992). The leader and faculty developer roles each account for 4 of the 12 most important tasks (tasks 2, 8, 10, and 12 and tasks 1, 3, 4, and 7, respectively), and 3 tasks represent the manager role (tasks 5, 6, and 11). Evidently, as faculty move into administration, they sacrifice their prior scholarship activities; only a single scholar task made the top-12 listing, that of remaining current within the academic discipline (task 9).

Ironically, chairs do not feel trained in or prepared for many of these important tasks. As Table 1.3 reflects, the chairs we surveyed said they needed training assistance with faculty evaluation (1), reducing conflicts among faculty (2), encouraging professional development activities for faculty (7), and recruiting and selecting faculty (12). Chapters 2 through 4 of this book will help you with these challenges. Then, chapters 5 through 7 will assist with your leadership and management training needs: obtaining funds (3), preparing and proposing budgets (4), developing and initiating long-range department goals (5), and managing department resources (6). Finally, chapter 8 addresses what frustrates chairs the most: not being able to keep current within their disciplines.

If you compare the most important tasks of department chairs listed in Table 1.2 with the tasks for which chairs feel the greatest need of training in Table 1.3, you will find that the items on the two lists are almost identical. There is no doubt that department chairs believe they are ill prepared for the important roles they are asked to assume.

Faculty Developer

First and foremost, department chairs view their faculty developer role as their most important responsibility. Australian researchers Moses and Roe (1990) asked faculty members what they believe are the most significant responsibilities of department chairs, and they responded in simi-

Table 1.2. Top 12 Tasks for Department Chairs

CHAIR TASKS	PERCENTAGE INDICATING HIGH IMPORTANCE*
1. Recruit and select faculty	93
2. Represent department to administration and the field	92
3. Evaluate faculty performance	90
4. Encourage faculty research and publication	89
5. Reduce conflict among faculty	88
6. Manage department resources	85
7. Encourage professional development of faculty	85
8. Develop and initiate long-range department goals	83
9. Remain current within academic discipline	78
10. Provide informal faculty leadership	75
11. Prepare and propose budgets	73
12. Solicit ideas to improve the department	71

SOURCE: Gmelch, Burns, et al. (1992).

*Percentage of high importance is determined by the proportion of chairs assigning the item a score of 4 or 5 on a 5-point Likert scale from 1 = low importance to 5 = high importance on 26 department chair tasks. Percentages ranged from 93% to 32%.

lar fashion—to help faculty achieve their potential. Whether in small liberal arts colleges or comprehensive research universities in the United States or elsewhere in the world, chairs understand their primary role (Sarros, Gmelch, and Tanewski 1997, 1998; Wolverton, Gmelch, et al. 1999). Faculty development involves not only the tasks of recruitment, selection, and evaluation of faculty but also the provision of informal leadership to enhance faculty teaching, morale, and professional development.

If you do not believe faculty development is your most important role, pull out your budget and calculate the proportion of funds you spend on personnel—most of you will find 85 to 90 percent of your department budgets allocated to faculty and staff salaries. Reflect on the top 12 tasks of department chairs in Table 1.2 for a moment and note the chair's number-one responsibility—faculty recruitment and selection.

Chapter 2 addresses in detail your role in recruiting new faculty. Remember, however, that in personnel selection, you have only three

Table 1.3. Training Needs for Department Chairs

1. Evaluate faculty performance

2. Reduce conflict among faculty

3. Obtain and manage external funds

4. Prepare and propose budgets

5. Develop and initiate long-range department goals

6. Manage department resources (finances, facilities, equipment)

7. Encourage professional development activities of faculty

8. Manage nonacademic staff

9. Plan and evaluate curriculum development

10. Provide informal faculty leadership

11. Ensure maintenance of accurate department records

12. Recruit and select faculty

SOURCE: Gmelch, Burns, et al. (1992).

choices. First, you can hire triple stars, those senior faculty who have already achieved success in teaching, scholarship, and service. Such stars are expensive, however, and they may not be within your budgetary constraints. Second, you can hire assistant professors and develop them into excellent teachers, scholars, and citizens—but this takes time, energy, and a plan of action. Finally, if you cannot afford to hire triple stars, and you do not have the time or resources to develop faculty, your third choice is —luck. You really have no choice but to hire superstars or to hire potential stars and develop them. Chapters 3 and 4 provide you with ideas about developing your faculty and the behaviors you need to exhibit in doing so, first by supporting their efforts and then by motivating them to succeed.

Manager

Acting as a manager, the foremost role of the chair from the dean's perspective, represents the chair's fiduciary requirement. Chairs spend more than half their time in any given week managing their departments, that is, performing maintenance functions: preparing budgets, maintaining department records, assigning duties to faculty, supervising nonacademic staff, and overseeing maintenance of finances, facilities, and equipment. Of the chairs we surveyed, 85 percent believe that "managing department resources" is very important, and 73 percent recognize the critical importance of "preparing and proposing budgets" (see tasks 6 and 11 in Table 1.2).

Ironically, although chairs recognize the importance of the manager role, they like this role least (McLaughlin, Montgomery, and Malpass 1975). Why, then, do they take the position of chair in the first place? Those who see themselves predominantly as managers say they accepted the position primarily to "take their turn" and that they strive to preserve homeostasis —if in fact preserving homeostasis can be said to be striving for anything. They are at a loss when asked to identify satisfiers associated with the position and complain of major difficulties from periodic uncertainty about future levels of funding and irritations stemming from central administration (Harris-Sledge 1994).

This portrayal of the managerial duties of department chairs weaves a necessary, but irritating, texture into their jobs. Chapters 5 and 6 will help you understand the nature of your managerial function and how to perform it effectively.

Leader

As leaders of their departments, chairs provide long-term direction and vision. They also provide external leadership for their departments by working with their constituents to coordinate department activities, represent their departments at professional meetings, and, on behalf of their departments, participate in college and university committees to keep faculty informed of external concerns. Chairs seem to like this role because of the challenges it affords and because of the opportunities it provides them, both to help others develop professional skills and to influence the profession and the department.

Chairs who identify themselves primarily as leaders find great satisfaction in leading capable, competitive teams of faculty, and they strive to promote their departments as outstanding and respected entities on campus. One of the most difficult parts of the leadership role involves keeping faculty and staff morale up as workloads increase. Overall, those identified as leader chairs demonstrate high levels of enthusiasm and energy toward their position (Harris-Sledge 1994). The leadership role of the chair is the topic of chapter 7.

Scholar

In contrast to the managerial nature of the three roles described thus far, chairs also try to retain their scholar identity while serving as chairs. This role includes the continuing need to teach and keep current in their academic disciplines and, for those in research universities, to maintain active research programs and obtain grants to support their research. Not surprisingly, many chairs enjoy and feel most comfortable in this role (McLaughlin, Montgomery, and Malpass 1975) but express frustration at their inability to spend much time pursuing their academic interests.

Table 1.4. Types of Department Chairs

- Department chairs who play instruments are musical chairs.

- Those who overdress are upholstered chairs.

- Those who kick back and do nothing are recliner chairs.

- Those who collapse under pressure are folding chairs.

- Those unsteady on their feet are rocking chairs.

- Those who lazily go through the motions are lounge chairs.

- Those who have no standards are easy chairs.

- Those who always complain are beach chairs.

- Those who write devastating reports are electric chairs.

- And those who dump on others are just plain stools.

SOURCE: Walter H. Gmelch, Iowa State University, College of Education

In fact, 88 percent of the chairs we surveyed reported that since becoming chairs, they spend less time with their research, writing, and keeping current with their disciplines, a condition of the chair position that causes great dissatisfaction and stress (Gmelch, Carroll, et al. 1990). To compound the issue, in addition to the four out of five chairs who spend less time "keeping current," only 39 percent reported having any degree of success at maintaining their effectiveness in scholarship (Carroll and Gmelch 1994).

This contradiction causes the number-one stress among department chairs: "having insufficient time to stay current in their academic fields" (Gmelch and Burns 1993). Most chairs would spend more time on their own academic endeavors if they could but find it virtually impossible because of the time required to perform their managerial duties. Therefore, as we have already noted, only 1 of the 12 most important tasks for chairs involves scholarship: that of remaining current within one's academic discipline. This theme recurs throughout this and other studies of the department chair and is in need of attention.

As we have seen, chairs lead complex lives. They prefer some duties of the job over others. Keep in mind the emphasis you place on these roles as you read the subsequent chapters of this book. Your challenge is to weave all four roles into a sturdy fabric worthy of wear. Remember, take your job seriously, but keep your perspective and humor. In an attempt to lighten up, review the types of department chairs given in Table 1.4.

Weaving Your Web

Before moving on to chapter 2, take a moment to assess how effective you are in each of the four roles by completing Exercise 1.1. This exercise is adapted from our previous book on strategic planning and how to manage department chair time, conflict, and stress (Gmelch and Miskin 1993). This current book complements our previous work by concentrating on how department chairs can fulfill their roles and build strong faculty and strong departments. After you have completed Exercise 1.1, the web you need to weave should become more evident to you.

As you begin to weave your four roles together, a note of caution is in order. It is tempting to "type" yourself as one kind of chair or another. Even if you see yourself as a certain chair type, however, you most likely possess a complex combination of skills and interests embedded in all four roles.

Exercise 1.1. Department Chair Role Orientation Instrument

CHAIR ROLE

A. Listed below are 24 typical duties of department chairs. Please answer how effective your performance is in each of the duties.

	Low				High

Leader

Coordinate department activities with constituents	1	2	3	4	5
Plan and evaluate curriculum development	1	2	3	4	5
Solicit ideas to improve the department	1	2	3	4	5
Represent the department at professional meetings	1	2	3	4	5
Inform faculty of department, college, and university concerns	1	2	3	4	5
Develop and initiate long-range department goals	1	2	3	4	5

Scholar

Obtain resources for personal research	1	2	3	4	5
Maintain research program and associated professional activities	1	2	3	4	5
Remain current within academic discipline	1	2	3	4	5
Obtain and manage external funds (grants, contracts)	1	2	3	4	5
Select and supervise graduate students	1	2	3	4	5
Teach and advise students	1	2	3	4	5

Faculty Developer

Encourage professional development efforts of faculty	1	2	3	4	5
Provide informal faculty leadership	1	2	3	4	5
Encourage faculty research and publication	1	2	3	4	5
Recruit and select faculty	1	2	3	4	5
Maintain conducive work climate, including reducing conflicts	1	2	3	4	5
Evaluate faculty performance	1	2	3	4	5

Manager

Prepare and propose budgets	1	2	3	4	5
Manage department resources (finances, facilities, equipment)	1	2	3	4	5
Ensure the maintenance of accurate department records	1	2	3	4	5
Manage nonacademic staff	1	2	3	4	5
Assign teaching, research, and other related duties to faculty	1	2	3	4	5
Write department reports and memos	1	2	3	4	5

DEPARTMENT CHAIR ROLE ORIENTATION INSTRUMENT SCORING

The Department Chair Role Orientation Instrument is keyed to four different roles department chairs perform.

B. Add your total score for each role. Plot your scores on the appropriate axes on the next page; then connect the points with straight lines to get a visual representation of the web you are weaving as a department chair. What are your dominant and backup chair roles?

Role

Leader _____   Faculty Developer _____
Scholar _____   Manager _____

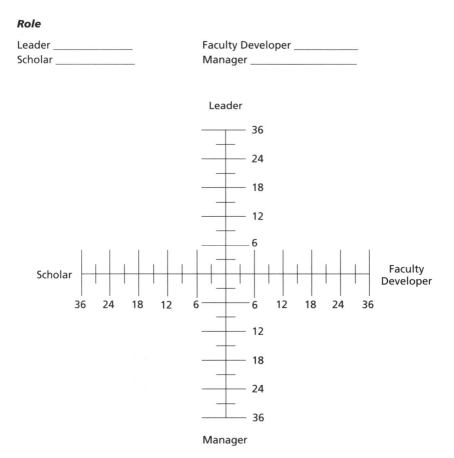

SOURCE: Reprinted with permission from *Leadership Skills for Department Chairs,* by Walter H. Gmelch and Val D. Miskin (pp. 12–13). Copyright 1993 by Anker Publishing Company, Inc.

PART I

FACULTY DEVELOPER

Chapter 2

RECRUIT QUALITY FACULTY

— The Million-Dollar Decision —

> There is something that is much
> more scarce, something rarer than
> ability. It is the ability to recognize ability.
> —Dennis Conner

The first thread forming the fabric of chair leadership is the development of productive faculty. Colleges and universities often pay lip service to the importance of faculty development. Chairs typically are rewarded for paying close attention to the managerial requirements imposed by their deans. How can you change the time and attention you spend on recruiting and developing your faculty? Chapters 2, 3, and 4 examine three critical behaviors necessary for building and maintaining productive faculty: selecting the right faculty, supporting their activities, and motivating their success. We offer this discussion of behaviors not simply as another list of actions but as a framework of behaviors necessary to your performance of the role of faculty developer (see Figure 2.1).

RECRUITMENT OF QUALITY FACULTY

No other decision in your department will be as important as the selection of a faculty colleague. Deliberate and careful selection of new colleagues has more to do with the growth and well-being of your department than any other action you may take. You are adding a family member to your department culture. Assuming that faculty exercise little mobility in their professional careers, the faculty you recruit today will be yours for life.

Figure 2.1. Faculty Development Molecule: Elements of Chair Behavior

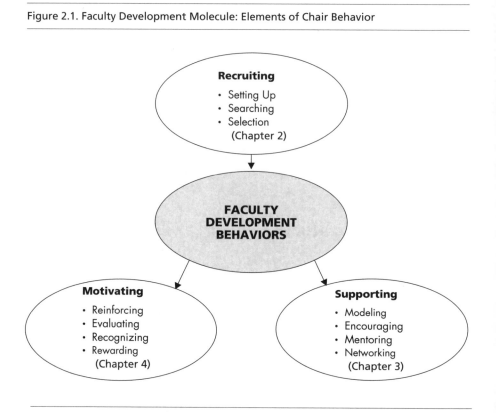

This is a million-dollar decision—both in terms of financial resources and in terms of psychic satisfaction. You cannot afford a bad decision, so you must make it carefully. The literature on faculty searches offers little consensus on exactly how to conduct an effective search. An excellent comprehensive handbook for recruiting administrators by Marchese and Lawrence (1989) provides some assistance, as does Rosse and Levin's more recent *Academic Administrator's Guide to Hiring* (2003). However, short of this, the tradition of simply placing an ad in the *Chronicle of Higher Education,* sitting back, and letting the applications roll in will not produce the results you want, especially if you want to attract the best-qualified candidates, including women and minorities.

The purpose of this chapter is to outline a practical set of procedures and options for conducting the search for and securing the most suitable faculty members for your department's needs. This requires a proactive, assertive, and positive approach. The wait-and-see, passive, laid-back strategy is insufficient.

THE SEARCH PROCESS

Although much of the search process follows the rituals, norms, and traditions of the particular institution, in this chapter we suggest effective search practices that you may find helpful to consider in your next recruitment effort. No matter what techniques and tips you may pick up along the way, four principles should guide your search: cost, centrality, importance, and need.

Cost

Not only are you investing in a million-dollar, lifelong decision, but the search process itself consumes indirect expenditures in terms of hundreds of faculty hours and chair time, as well as the direct expenses of advertising, travel, and materials.

In terms of time, searches are traditionally initiated in the fall and not ended until sometime in the spring—approximately seven months to fill one position. Selection processes in the private sector differ significantly and appear to be more efficient, especially when candidates can be selected or promoted from within an organization. However, institutions of higher education rarely fill vacancies with their own graduates, for fear of "inbreeding." Overall, the recruitment process in higher education takes longer than it does in the private sector, generates a larger pool of candidates, and involves many more committees, person hours, and constituents.

Centrality

Department chairs are likely to be measured by the quality of their faculty appointments. In fact, studies conducted by the Center for the Study of Academic Leadership[1] show that chairs often comment, when asked what they would like to be remembered for, that they want to be known as chairs who developed a "quality department through selection of faculty."

Although department chairs cannot take sole responsibility for the recruitment of faculty, active recruitment of first-rate faculty is their primary responsibility. From a candidate's point of view, the department should appear attractive, supportive, challenging, and satisfying to personal and professional ambitions. The chair must create a clear and convincing case that these challenges and satisfactions can be found in his or her particular department.

---

1 The Center for the Study of the Department Chair changed its name in 1998 to the Center for the Study of Academic Leadership, under the charter of the University Council for Educational Administration. The revised Center has expanded its research endeavors to include those of academic deans and other academic leaders.

Importance

"Given the lack of mobility in most areas of our academic profession, one should select a colleague with only slightly less care than choosing a spouse. In fact, comparing tenure rates with divorce rates reveals that a choice of an academic colleague may well be more important" (Hynes 1990, 52). This statement highlights the importance of the faculty hiring decision. The analogy to marriage reminds us of the old adage that you can't select your relatives, but you can select your friends. You need to select your faculty friends carefully, as they will have direct impacts on your academic culture and department productivity.

Need

More than half of the faculty members in the 3,200 institutions of higher education in the United States will retire in the next decade. Given the expected needs of the colleges and universities that will be losing such large numbers, how can department chairs effectively recruit and hire faculty to maintain department excellence and promote multiple perspectives through the active recruitment of minority group members and women?

Although the search process you employ in your institution may be based on your institution's type and traditions, this chapter can still provide you with a road map of the search process. No single model universally fits all college searches, and most colleges follow fairly well defined procedures for hiring.

Some of these procedures may assist you merely with complying with state and federal regulations. You can give life to your college's search process by applying a proactive approach. Be aware of the following conditions and constraints in your selection process:

- Candidate selection is extremely time consuming.
- The development of criteria against which candidates will be compared is vital to selecting the right person.
- For a successful search result, it is critical to assess and achieve a fit between the department's needs and the candidate's abilities.
- The process must be open and candid among colleagues and those affected by the hiring.
- Although the dean may make the final selection, it is you, as department chair, who must champion the search to develop the strongest and most diverse pool possible. Your reputation and success depend on it.

- Remember that selection is a two-way process—the candidate must want to work at your institution if you want a successful relationship.
- Your role as department chair may be either to head up the search personally or, at a minimum, to stay in close contact with the search committee.

THE FACULTY SELECTION CYCLE

The search cycle may be viewed as a three-stage process for faculty selection and subsequent steps within each stage (see Figure 2.2). Each of these stages resembles a program that, once completed, leads to the next stage, regresses to an earlier stage, or repeats the same stage.

STAGE 1: IDENTIFICATION—THE SETUP

Focus on Department Planning

The search for a new colleague provides you with a critical opportunity to improve and augment the department in relation to your status in the institution, relationship to the field, and competitiveness in your discipline. Usually, your search will occur in the wake of dialogue with your dean and members of your department regarding the merits of your department's needs within the context of the university or college. Although normal practice suggests you identify department goals and needs prior to initiating the search, in practice you may find that the search itself creates an opportunity to revisit and redefine your goals. In fact, department goals may change every time you hire new faculty members.

Recruitment of faculty members should not be done in isolation but as an integral part of the department's mission and consistent with a clearly established set of department goals. A thorough examination of your department's needs begins with an assessment of the institution's place within higher education. Not all institutions claim the same goals and identities. Research and doctoral-granting institutions may place greater emphasis on research, whereas liberal arts institutions and community colleges may concentrate more on teaching, and others may serve their own particular market niches. Your department's faculty openings should be created in concert with the mission and needs of your department. In addition, every department has a certain character, tone, or culture. Some may represent family values of collaboration and dependency, whereas others may be highly competitive and individualistic. Departments should also take stock of the existing faculty specializations and competencies as well as particular client groups, such as students, private industry, and government agencies.

Figure 2.2. Faculty Development Molecule: Faculty Selection Cycle

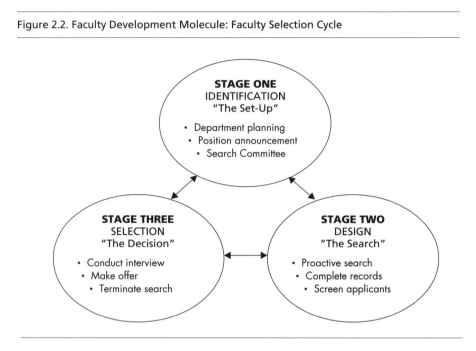

Both the institution's and the department's unique identity must be conveyed in the job announcement. Before you craft the job description, you should answer the following questions:

- What is your institution's place in higher education?
- What is your department's place in the institution?
- What expertise or specializations already exist among your faculty members?
- What do your customers and students expect to receive from your department?
- How would you characterize the unique qualities your department has to offer?
- What can you afford in terms of faculty rank, salary, benefits, and extraordinary incentives?

The discussion in chapter 6 should assist you in framing your responses to these questions. Once you have answered these questions, you are ready to move on to the next step: designing the job announcement.

Design the Job Announcement

Once your department has assessed the context of the search, you must create a description of the position to be filled. You need to prepare two kinds of descriptions. The first is a short statement, usually placed as an ad in a variety of media. The second is a longer, more elaborate, full description that can be sent to professional associations, faculty colleagues, chairs in other institutions, and prospective candidates.

Prepare your job announcement from the following list of specifications. Do not bury these specifications—make them clear and easy to find.

1. Description and name of your department and institution, including the following:

   • mission statement

   • particular clientele served

   • degrees and/or certificates granted

2. Academic rank of the opening

3. Minimum qualifications, such as desired degree and experience required

4. Special characteristics or expertise desired, such as areas of specialization, ability to work in a team environment

5. Description of teaching, research, and service responsibilities

6. Appointment status—tenure or term appointment

7. Employment status—academic or calendar year

8. Salary range or statement of salary competitiveness with peer institutions

9. Starting date of applicant screening

10. Starting date of employment

11. Statement of special considerations encouraging minorities and women

12. How to apply, including name, address, and telephone number of contact person and application requirements, such as placement file and current letters of recommendation

Exhibit 2.1 displays a sample job announcement with reference in brackets to each of the 12 specifications suggested here. A shorter version of the job announcement can be used in advertisements such as the ones found in the *Chronicle of Higher Education*. The longer version should elaborate all of the information needed; it will be used to market the position and to sell your department and institution to prospective candidates. It will also allow potential candidates to screen themselves out if they do not perceive an appropriate match between their skills and backgrounds and the conditions and requirements of your position.

Exhibit 2.1. Sample Position Announcement

---

[1] **Department of Educational Leadership and Policy Studies
Position Announcement**

[2] **Higher Education Administration and Leadership Studies
Open Rank**

POSITION:
Leadership Studies and Higher Education. Rank is open. Full-time, tenure-track [6], academic year (9-month) appointment [7]. Appointment effective August 16, 2005 [10]. Screening of applicants begins February 1, 2005 [9].

[4] **RESPONSIBILITIES:**
Responsibilities include (a) teaching a variety of graduate courses in higher education administration, as well as courses in support of an interdisciplinary undergraduate minor in leadership studies; (b) conducting ongoing scholarly research leading to publication in areas of individual specialization; (c) developing and maintaining collaborative relationships with the higher education community; and (d) advising undergraduate students in the education leadership program and graduate students in the higher education programs.

[3] **QUALIFICATIONS:**
Qualifications include (a) an earned doctorate in educational leadership, higher education, or a closely related field; (b) record of excellence in teaching at the college level; (c) either a record of scholarly publication or, for consideration at the assistant professor level, potential to establish an individual research [5] agenda that will lead to tenure and promotion (qualification for graduate faculty status—three refereed publications—is preferred); and (d) theoretical and methodological expertise in the area of higher education and leadership studies. Preference may be given to candidates with prior administration experience in higher education and/or experience in undergraduate leadership development.

[11] The department is particularly interested in appointing an individual who will enhance our efforts to address ethnic and cultural diversity issues, as well as our efforts to build collaborative relationships with the institution's constituencies.

[8] **SALARY:**
Salary is commensurate with experience.

[12] **APPLICATION PROCESS:**
Persons wishing to apply for this position should send a letter of application addressing the qualification criteria; three current letters of recommendation addressing this specific position; samples of two scholarly works; evidence of quality teaching; and a current comprehensive vita including the names, addresses, and phone numbers of at least three additional references to: Dr. John S. Schuh, Chair, Department of Educational Leadership and Policy Studies, Iowa State University, Ames, IA 50011, Website: www.iastate.edu.

Most institutions routinely advertise their openings in a variety of media, the most appropriate being the *Chronicle of Higher Education*. Ads in the *Chronicle* are necessary for all searches, but not sufficient. If you are interested in increasing underrepresented groups, you will need to augment these advertisements with other recruiting activities, the second stage of the recruitment process. However, the next step, selection of a diverse search committee, precedes any solitary action by the chair. You may even want to get the search committee involved in developing the job description.

Select the Search Committee

The use of search and screening committees is relatively new in higher education, but over the past 25 years it has become the norm. Committee representation should be diverse enough to cover the interests of your department, your clientele group, department stakeholders, and the broader community but at the same time should represent the best interests of ethnic and gender diversity.

The composition of the committee symbolically and substantively represents the internal and external interests of your program. This is not to say that search committee members should not also be knowledgeable about your program, but foremost, they should represent all departmental constituencies. As John Murray (1993, 17) suggests:

> No matter how well you implement [the first stage], your efforts will be instantly annihilated if the make-up of the hiring committee is not carefully considered. Too many colleges make the mistake of repeatedly naming the same individuals, . . . ones who work well together, . . . share the same ideology. . . . However, balancing a committee for differences in attitude or philosophy is of paramount importance and much more difficult. It takes a departmental or institutional leader with courage and insight to put together a committee that accurately reflects the tensions that should exist.

Simply put, if two committee members always agree, maybe one of them is unnecessary.

The challenge placed before the search committee usually comes in the form of a letter from the dean asking members to serve. The letter should also outline the selection criteria, special considerations such as diversity, and tasks of the committee, which usually include the following:

1. Developing the position announcement and marketing strategy

2. Paper screening of all candidate applications

3. Contacting references as appropriate

4. Conducting interviews

5. Presenting a report to the dean or chair outlining the strengths and limitations of the final list of candidates

Instructions from the dean or chair should be clear from the beginning, whether the committee is just searching and screening or searching, screening, and selecting/ranking final choices. Most deans will ask for unranked lists of acceptable and unacceptable candidates from those interviewed. Instructions concerning who will make the final selection should be clear, so as to avoid misleading and frustrating the search committee. Candidates must also be evaluated according to the selection criteria. Ranking of the final candidates may also cause embarrassment if the candidate who accepts the position ends up being the second or third choice because other top choices declined to accept or withdrew. A good working relationship with the dean and provost will resolve most of these concerns.

Stage 2: Design—The Search

Search Proactively

The search must be launched in an active, assertive, and positive manner to generate an excellent pool of faculty candidates. Consider the applicant's point of view. Your institution must appear attractive, worthwhile, and able to provide an opportunity for advancement; otherwise, the best applicants will not waste their time. Make an effort to describe and market your campus and the culture of your department. Active marketing can take many forms.

1. *Broaden the scope of your advertisements.* As previously suggested, the placement of your short and long vacancy notices is important. Almost exclusively, the short notice is usually written for an advertisement in the *Chronicle of Higher Education.* You might also consider advertising in the metropolitan newspapers of cities known to have significant populations of minority and women scholars. You may augment your exposure and potentially increase your candidate pool through strong academic marketplace publications with special niches for minority members or women, such as *The Black Scholar;* through professional associations, such as the American Psychological Association, the University Council for Educational Administration, and the American Educational Research Association; and through other publicity channels within your discipline, such as newsletters in your field.

2. *Use all existing networks to find prime candidates.* Do not conduct a passive search, simply placing ads in the appropriate professional publications. Actively use your network of fellow department chairs, professional

associations, and previous contacts to seek out the best candidates. With respect to minority recruitment especially, contact previous visitors to campus and minority administrators, alumni, and friends to recruit actively from underrepresented groups. Learn to recognize predominantly black colleges and universities and establish contacts within their programs or build a minority presence through faculty exchanges or minority student teaching fellowships. We offered summer minority teaching fellowships at our institution with the hope that someday we might be in a position to hire one of the former fellows or to ask for assistance in identifying potential candidates.

3. *Use your campus culture and environment to your advantage.* Perhaps the appeal of your campus is a "well-kept secret." Apply some introspection and identify what makes your campus or department unique, and then market your specialty to professionals who may find a good match between what they want and what you have to offer. For example, do not assume that minority candidates will not want to teach in a predominantly white institution.

4. *Make sure your affirmative action statement reflects your dedication to underrepresented groups.* It helps if in your ad there is something unusual about your stance on affirmative action—something beyond the typical perfunctory statement about being "an equal opportunity employer." Such static wording suggests compliance with the letter, but not the spirit, of the law. For example, you might include a statement such as the following: "The department is particularly interested in appointing an individual who will enhance our efforts to address ethnic and cultural diversity issues, as well as our efforts to build collaborative relationships with the institution's constituencies."

Keep Complete and Accurate Records

To maintain an objective and efficient process, you should designate someone in your office to manage the operation of the search process —specifically to process the papers, mail out routine correspondence to applicants, and so on. This staff assistant should track the entire recruitment process, from the mailing of the announcements to the submission of the final appointment papers. Each application should be kept in an individual folder with a checklist attached indicating the status of the application. At an appropriate time, you should acknowledge each application in writing: Thank the applicant for his or her interest in the position, restate your time line, and inform the applicant of the status of the application (e.g., whether all materials and references have been received, what is still outstanding). A master list of all the applicants indicating their demographic data (name, gender, ethnicity, degrees, and locations) can be prepared by your search assistant for distribution to the committee members

Figure 2.3. Sample Candidate Comparison Sheet

Number	Name	Vitae	Letters of Recommendation	Sex (M or F)	Degree	Date of Degree	Institution	Experience	Publications	Professional Organizations

and the office of affirmative action shortly after the closing date (see the example in Figure 2.3).

Each applicant's folder usually contains a cover letter of application, curriculum vitae, letters of reference, and miscellaneous supporting material. As you review each of these pieces of evidence, scrutinize them with the following questions in mind:

1. Does the cover letter clearly address the job description established for the position?

2. Does the vita clearly communicate the qualifications and responsibilities you need to paper screen the applicant? Are there gaps in the applicant's employment record that are not explained? Is the vita constructed in such a way that it raises suspicion or doubt about the real achievements of the applicant?

3. Are the letters of reference current? Do they directly address the job requirements of your opening? Who wrote them? Do not take letters of reference at face value, particularly those prepared by candidates' advisers.

4. Is the supplemental material necessary and well organized, or does it convey a lack of organization and vision by the applicant?

Note that you should take an applicant's cover letter of application as seriously as his or her curriculum vitae. Many times a cover letter can reveal a person's writing skills and ability to address directly the criteria you have outlined in the job announcement. A stock letter designed to be sent to all institutions does not reflect a candidate who is very serious about your opening.

Devise a standard evaluation or rating sheet for committee members to use in assessing the candidates' qualifications as outlined in the job announcement. You might consider having the committee members turn their rating forms for all candidates over to the office assistant, who can summarize them on a matrix to be used in the initial screening meeting.

Screen the Applicants

The Initial Screening Meeting

The committee's first real work is to review the applications in the pool. Usually, the pool is so large that comparison and evaluation of all candidates are difficult and time consuming. However, having all members of the search committee review each file serves two purposes: (a) the search committee members assure themselves that no outstanding candidates have been overlooked, and (b) in the review of all candidates, some who may not initially appear attractive may surface within the context of the entire pool of applicants.

Some colleges and universities have developed elaborate sets of procedures for screening applicants; others operate at the other extreme, being more casual and informal in their approach. The method you use depends on both your institutional requirements and your department's style. Probably somewhere between being overbureaucratic and laissez-faire lies the most effective screening approach. On the one hand, a clear set of procedures ensures a certain level of objectivity and thoroughness. However, without flexibility and intuitive insight, the screening process can become entangled with restrictive and regulatory processes. Your screening procedures should provide you with the following (Hynes 1990):

1. Guidelines and criteria for reviewing applicants' folders

2. Designation of persons authorized to speak with the applicants and their references

3. A schedule of information needed from the candidates at various levels of consideration (initial pool, semifinalists, finalists)

4. A definition of the relationship between the search committee and the dean

5. An outline of the activities that will occur when candidates interview for the job

From the record keeping of your staff, you should prepare a candidate comparison matrix on which each rater's comments are reported anonymously. This may help develop consensus at the first meeting as to what action to take on each applicant. After assessing each candidate on every criterion, screening committee members usually place the candidate in one of three categories: advance, hold, or eliminate. Thus, the committee will look for consensus on the action for each candidate.

Once the committee has agreed on the candidates it wishes to advance or eliminate in the first round, either by consensus or by vote, your task is to determine the action you wish to take with the candidates who are marginal or in the "hold" position. When the committee is forced to agree or develop consensus on these candidates, several things can happen. First, committee members may find they need to undertake more careful examination of the candidates' credentials, which will either enhance or detract from the candidates' desirability. Second, the committee may find it needs to be clearer about the actual meanings of heuristic criteria used in the job description, such as "successful prior teaching experience" or "an established record of scholarship." This process of discovering the actual meanings of the criteria is part of the retrospective sense-making through which the committee begins to define, after the fact, the criteria on which they base the selection of candidates to advance to the next stage (Birnbaum 1988). Although you may use an elaborate system for rating and ranking candidates, giving the appearance of objectivity and accuracy, a great deal of discussion among committee members is required before everyone understands the true meanings of the numbers used to rank candidates.

Finally, to narrow down a list of potential applicants, the search committee may look for disqualifying characteristics. This represents a process different from searching for reasons to keep candidates in the pool. For applicants who are not advanced, the committee might want to devise elimination codes, such as the ones suggested in the following list, to ensure objectivity and consistency in the process. Such codes can also be useful for explaining the process when you submit your list of finalists to the dean and office of affirmative action.

Candidate's disqualification

    C-1:   Failed to provide minimum components of application

    C-2:   Failed to respond to requests for additional information

Degree consideration

    D-1:   Did not possess required degree as advertised

    D-2:   Degree not in compatible field with needs of department

Teaching requirements

    T-1:   Area of specialization overlaps with current faculty

    T-2:   Candidate's teaching not suitable

Research/scholarship requirements

R-l: Insufficient publication (exhibition/performance) record

R-2: Lack of demonstrated research/performance skills

R-3: Not published adequately given length of time in profession

The committee should keep in mind the department's and institution's diversity goals when reviewing applications and should retain as many individuals from underrepresented groups as possible for consideration in the second screening process. The goal of the initial screening is to reduce the field of candidates to a reasonable number for the first set of calls to references. Usually, 10 to 15 applicants will emerge for further screening.

After the Initial Screening

At this point, it is always a sound practice to have the search committee inform the candidates that they have made your "long list" and that you will be making calls to their references. This may also provide an important opportunity to conduct short telephone interviews with the candidates. From these discussions, the committee may get a feel for candidates' oral communication abilities as well as their interests and motives for applying to your institution.

Some search committees use an additional paper screening method at this point by asking candidates on the long list to submit personal philosophy statements. These give the committee additional data on the candidates' writing skills as well as their seriousness in seeking the position. You may also wish to send each candidate on the long list a packet of materials on your department, institution, and community at this time, so the candidate can better assess the fit between his or her needs and what you have to offer. Remember, however, that this extra screening process will lengthen your search by an additional two to three weeks.

Making Reference Calls

Once a reasonable number of applicants have been screened, committee members should begin making calls to the candidates' references. Researchers have found that phone references are particularly important sources for establishing the credibility and reliability of information provided by applicants. It is a good idea to have at least two committee members call references on each candidate, so no one member becomes a champion or detractor for any one candidate. At least three or four calls should be made on each candidate.

Go beyond the list of references the candidate has provided (as a courtesy, you should inform the candidate you will be seeking additional sources). A standardized list of telephone reference check questions will help committee members to get consistent types of information on all candidates (see Figure 2.4). However, references should also be given time to elaborate beyond answering your standard questions about the candidate's strengths and needed areas of growth. In addition, any questions concerning unique qualities that have emerged from the committee discussion should be asked at this point. As a final question, the committee member should ask for the names of additional persons the committee might contact who are not already listed as references by the applicant.

The Final Screening

The next screening committee meeting should center on the data generated by the reference checks made concerning candidates on the long list. You will now want to narrow down your field to the final three or four persons you wish to invite for interviews. As a result of the reference checks, some of the candidates may drop completely from consideration. Try to get your committee to develop some ranking of the candidates, so it is easier for you to review and submit your list of top candidates for interview to the dean. The object of this meeting is to develop consensus on a list of candidates who will be clearly acceptable to the faculty, chair, and dean.

In the transmittal memo to the dean, outline the strengths and weaknesses of each candidate and address the reasons for any minority or women applicants not included in your final list. Make sure you have checked the credentials of those candidates you wish to interview. Now is the time, before you spend the resources and money for a campus visit, to verify degrees obtained, to ask for explanations in employment gaps, to check any inconsistencies in applicants' files, and to try to get more diversity. Also, reflect again on whether the candidates' qualifications and career objectives compare with the department's mission and expectations. Make sure your screening process has not compromised your department's requirements.

It is safe and professionally proper at this time to send letters to those applicants who have been eliminated and will not receive further consideration. Those "on hold" should be retained until the third part of the selection cycle is complete. Remember, you may need to repeat or regress to Stage 2 if an impasse is reached in Stage 3.

Stage 3: Selection—The Million-Dollar Decision

Conduct the Interview and Visitation

The interview is the most important part of the faculty search process, yet most department chairs and search committees are not trained or prepared to conduct effective interviews. For example, attempts to conduct

---

Figure 2.4. Sample Standardized Form for Telephone Reference Checks

---

SEARCH
Educational Leadership and Policy Studies

Nominee/Candidate _____

Reference Contacted   Name: _____

                                     Title: _____

                                     Address: _____

                                     _____

Contacted by: _____   Date: _____

SUGGESTED QUESTIONS TO ASK WHEN TALKING TO REFERENCES

Introduction

This call is a confidential request for information on _____ , who is being considered by Iowa State University for the position of assistant/associate professor, Department of Educational Leadership and Policy Studies in the College of Education. We would appreciate any information you may be willing to provide to us, and we shall consider such information to be of a confidential nature.

1. How do you evaluate _____'s effectiveness in
   (a) building a record of distinction in the education profession as a professional educator?
   (b) evidence of commitment to the field of educational administration?
   (c) building a record of scholarly accomplishment in research?
   (d) working with teachers, education specialists, and administrators in public schools and colleges?
   (e) specialized knowledge and competency in areas of specialization?
   (f) graduate teaching in educational administration?

Comments on Effectiveness

2. Do _____'s colleagues, in your opinion, share these views on his/her effectiveness?

3. How do you rate _____'s attributes in the areas of
   (a) advising graduate students?
   (b) commitment to innovation?
   (c) enthusiasm?
   (d) interpersonal relations? with faculty? with students? with other administrators? with external public?
   (e) commitment to affirmative action?

4. What would be the impact if the candidate were to leave his/her present position?

5. Do you believe, considering all things, that _____ would be a good professor of educational administration?

6. Would you please identify for us others who may know the candidate and who might be contacted? [GET NAMES, ADDRESSES, AND TELEPHONE NUMBERS, IF POSSIBLE.]

---

off-campus interviews at professional association conference meetings are fraught with unkept appointments, time constraints, and inappropriate interview settings, such as coffee shops and bars. At best, an interview conducted away from your campus should be considered a "first look" for both you and the candidate, to see if a marriage of your interests and needs is possible. The professional conference interview provides the advantage of allowing you to check each other out, but it is no substitute for the campus visit.

The official campus visit invitation should be extended by the chair of the department and followed up by a letter of confirmation. At this time, you may wish to divulge more about the pay range, possible rank, and other vital data. This is also a time to check the candidate's sincere interest regarding your institution and position. Usually, all travel and per diem expenses are covered by the institution. However, to discourage candidates from shopping around solely to boost their positions back home, some colleges and universities in these difficult economic times now inform candidates that they will have to cover their own expenses if they are offered a position and decline to accept it. Although you do not want your institution to appear cheap, this seems to be a reasonable policy given the current political and economic climate in higher education.

The format for the interview process should be the same for each candidate. It will involve one to two days of intense experience for both the candidate and the institution. A typical interview schedule includes private meetings with the department chair, the dean, the search committee, and the faculty, as well as a presentation to students and faculty. We strongly suggest that you also include a campus tour, a real estate tour of your community, and private sessions with students, department staff, and your clientele and alumni. And don't forget to take advantage of the more relaxed opportunities you will have over meals, driving to and from the airport, and even during department socials to get to know your candidates.

The key is to solicit as many perspectives as possible. Make sure that you systematically collect written evaluations of each interview from all parties involved for the committee to use in its final deliberations. The form can be as simple as "Rate the candidate and indicate strengths and weaknesses he or she would bring to the department" or as directive as the following questions:

1. Does the candidate look better on paper than in person? If so, what personal characteristics contributed to a negative impression?

2. How did the candidate's energy level appear? Active? Average? Lethargic?

3. Did the candidate's body stance give the impression that he or she was nervous, relaxed, unsure, confused, defensive, or rigid?

4. What was seen in the candidate's facial expressions? Openness? Arrogance? Puzzlement? Pleasantness? Boredom? Alertness?

5. Were the expected weaknesses of the candidate confirmed by the interview?

6. Were the strengths confirmed? Were new strengths revealed? Did the candidate show genuine promise?

7. Did the interview reveal any unexpected problems? (Tucker 1992, 175)

One of the weakest areas of the interview process for untrained committees is in the questions asked. Many times, interview sessions are filled with rhetorical questions or statements on the part of committee members who are attempting to impress candidates with their own stature in the department or the prowess of department faculty. Obviously, the candidate must leave with a positive impression of the institution and faculty. However, the committee should use the interview process to solicit as much information as possible from candidates about their expertise, interests, and personal desires. To do this, interviewers should avoid closed-ended questions such as, "Did you apply to this department because you like to teach?" More useful are open-ended or behaviorally anchored questions that elicit responses illuminating the candidate's true interests, feelings, and character, such as, "In what ways have you demonstrated leadership?" and "What motivated you to apply for this particular position?" On the other hand, you must avoid asking questions that violate the rights of candidates or fair employment practices. For example, it is unlawful to ask candidates about their religious preferences, spouse's employment, health, or other non-job-related matters. Most colleges and universities have handbooks on interviewing available that will help you discriminate between appropriate and inappropriate questions.

Overall, you and the candidate should share the same interest—to see each other as you are. A certain degree of formality and pressure will always exist in any interview process, but many institutions have protocols designed to put candidates at ease so they can interview under the best circumstances. In *The Art of Administration,* Ken Eble (1978, 109) points out that "a good interview should range beyond the expected questions about degrees, areas of specialization, plans for scholarship, preferences in teaching, and the like into questions about why the prospect has chosen teaching and scholarship in the first place and how his or her professional life may relate to personal and community concerns."

Make the Offer

At this point, one hopes, you have congruence among the dean, the search committee, and you, as chair, on your top choice. If this is not the case, one of several alternatives may occur: (a) the person with the power makes the decision (in most cases, this means the dean), (b) to resolve the impasse you have to revert back to Stage 2 of the search cycle, or (c) you abandon the search and start over the next year—a costly alternative, but better than making the wrong million-dollar decision.

The most critical moment in a proactive search is the challenge of hiring your first choice. To capture this moment, you must have an understanding of the needs of the person you wish to employ. Throughout the interview process, you should have been listening for the candidate to express his or her personal and professional needs. Your objective is to match your top candidate's needs with what you can realistically offer. For example, you should be able to answer the following questions:

- Is your candidate's spouse in need of employment? If so, are there employment opportunities available in your community?
- What type of schooling is needed for the candidate's children?
- What does the candidate need to reach his or her five-year professional goals?
- What type of housing does the candidate desire?
- What are the candidate's interests in teaching, research, and service?
- What shortcomings might the candidate perceive to be inherent in your institution?
- What is the candidate's need for collegiality? For autonomy?
- What type of start-up costs will be incurred by the candidate's needs in terms of computers, labs, and research assistance?
- What needs might exist in terms of consulting or overload pay?

Do not think of the "offer" purely in terms of base salary. Further questions you should think about include the following: What kind of package can you put together in terms of tangible and intangible items? How comprehensive is your benefits package? Is your retirement system compatible with the candidate's current policy? What inducements can you provide in terms of moving expenses, summer session appointments, or overload pay for extra teaching? On the other hand, are you able to provide some extras such as reduced teaching load for beginning professors, student assistants for research, professional travel funds, personal computing start-up costs, and/or research laboratory space? The candidate may also be persuaded to accept your offer based on intangible advantages, such as the quality of life in your community, the reputation of the local public schools, opportunity for spousal accommodation or employment in your community, positive work environment, and interpersonal compatibility or collegiality of your faculty. Throughout the interview and negotiation process, give your candidate every chance to make a positive, but realistic, assessment of the total offer, including both tangible and intangible opportunities.

Once the offer is made, reconfirm it in writing, and ask your candidate to respond within a reasonable time, usually a week to 10 days. If the offer is accepted, an official contract is sent to the candidate to be signed and returned. Don't forget to have your staff assistant follow up with the institutional bureaucracy to make sure that appointment papers, payroll forms, and immigration visas, if applicable, are all in order for the candidate's arrival. You may also want to assist your new faculty member personally with his or her housing needs and arrangements regarding children's schooling and other basic issues, to help him or her make an easier transition into the new community.

Terminate the Search

Once a contract has been signed, you will need to send letters to the other applicants indicating that you have found the person you believe best meets the needs of the department. Thank them for their interest, and wish them well in their future endeavors. Generally, the records of the search should be kept in your archives for three to five years.

One final caveat to department chairs about recruiting faculty. This is only the beginning of an exhausting, but rewarding, process. Selecting faculty is your first step in building a productive department. Your next tasks, as discussed in the next two chapters, are to support their talents and advocate their advancement.

Chapter 3

SUPPORT YOUR FACULTY

— 80 Percent of Your Resources —

> In baseball and business, the needs
> of the team are best met when we meet
> the needs of the individual [players].
> —Max DePree

As we noted in chapter 2, no other decision you make will be as important as the selection of your department's faculty. Deliberate and careful selection of new colleagues has more to do with the development of your department than any other action you may take. Assuming that faculty members exercise little mobility in their professional careers, the selection of a new faculty member is a million-dollar decision. However, faculty selection without faculty development is like buying a new Mercedes and leaving it in the garage to collect dust, go out of style, and become obsolete. You need to fuel the car up and get it running.[1]

Will supportive behaviors on the part of the department chair directly increase faculty performance? Research on this subject has been both inconsistent and without firm conclusions. However, we do know that the support of superiors contributes to increased confidence, decreased stress, and increased cooperation in workers (Yukl 1994)—all productive faculty behaviors you should nurture. Consider the following four effective forms of supporting behaviors you can use to foster productivity in your faculty: modeling, motivating, mentoring, and networking.

---

1 Portions of chapters 3 and 4 have been adapted and expanded from W. H. Gmelch, "The Department Chair's Role in Improving Teaching," in *Improving College Teaching,* ed. Peter Seldin. Copyright 1995 by Anker Publishing Company, Inc.

Modeling Productive Behavior

Faculty perform better when they have the opportunity to observe others being productive. Help faculty get together with colleagues for any number of opportunities to model effective teaching, scholarship, and service. For example, ask faculty members to observe each other's teaching methods, or invite them to get involved in a community activity. The objective is for them to pick up ideas, techniques, and support from each other.

Another way to model productive behavior is to join faculty members in an interdisciplinary group of colleagues engaged in a project. When we first started our research on faculty stress, we invited three colleagues from political science, business, and sociology to form a study group. Not only did we all enjoy working together, but our ideas became synergistic as we observed a common problem from multiple perspectives, an interdisciplinary paradigm—a sociologist's, behavioral scientist's, and political scientist's model. In this case we had a common problem for discussion and compared our approaches on how to study it. Such an interdisciplinary approach to teaching, scholarship, and service can help individuals to break out of personal paradigms and provides refreshing modeling relationships. Get faculty involved in interdisciplinary research teams, and provide them with incentives to work collaboratively rather than in isolation. We learn from each other.

Finally, whenever you or faculty attend seminars, workshops, or conference presentations, you should keep separate sets of notes about teaching methods you observe and then share these tips with students and colleagues back home. Once, the first author attended a two-week seminar on management development conducted by a host of highly effective presenters. During the seminar, he kept two separate sets of notes, one on the content of the sessions and the other on the effective teaching techniques he observed during the seminar. Upon returning to his campus, he started to change some of its management practices in addition to revamping his class based on the teaching tips he picked up.

Motivating Performance

When asked to identify the most important role a chair plays in supporting faculty, one chair responded that it is to help faculty keep the stress and aggravation out of their lives. Job stress contributes to poor relations with colleagues, absenteeism, and loss of self-confidence and self-esteem. But some stress motivates faculty to perform better, just as athletes need stress in order to succeed (Gmelch 1993).

Interestingly, motivation and productivity decline when stress reaches either an excessive or an insufficient level. Note the basic orienta-

Figure 3.1. The Stress and Performance Curve

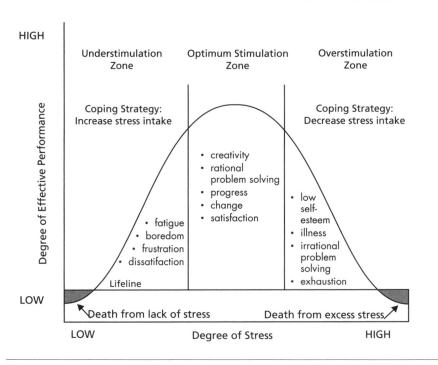

SOURCE: Adapted from Gmelch (1993).

tion of stress and performance in Figure 3.1. Stress ranges from low to high along the horizontal axis; performance ranges from low to high on the vertical axis. The relationship between stress and productivity, when graphed, translates into an inverted U-shaped curve; the level of performance increases as stress increases, up to a point, and then performance declines with further increases in stress.

Thus the stress-productivity research suggests that an optimum level of motivation is required to maximize performance. Those faculty who are understimulated suffer from the trauma of routine and uneventfulness —underchallenged and suffering from boredom, fatigue, frustration, and dissatisfaction with their faculty roles. Faculty functioning at this level may be said to rust out from lack of motivation. Their skills and/or knowledge have become obsolete. At the other extreme are faculty who have been working too hard for too long and who find themselves burned out. Here we find the ambitious, aggressive, and impatient faculty who have become exhausted from teaching too many classes, dissatisfied because they have not seen results from their scholarship, and despondent over their loss of self-esteem and the esteem of their colleagues.

Notice in Figure 3.1 the horizontal "lifeline" slightly above the base of the graph. The lifeline connotes low to no performance owing to too little or too much stress—no motivation. These are extreme points. On the left side, recall some faculty who have taught the same courses for the past 15 years and have never made any attempt to update or renew their material. They may be physically alive, but they are professionally dead. At the other extreme, you may recognize some faculty who have worked too long and too hard and now have gone beyond the burnout stage, to a point where they are neither physically or professionally "alive" with their scholarship—but remember, in order to be burned out, one must once have been on fire.

Does all this sound fictitious? In our study of stress and productivity, faculty teaching, research, and service performance resembled the stress and performance curve. With either too little stress (rust out) or too much stress (burnout), faculty performance declined, and only at moderate levels of stress did faculty report excellence in teaching, research, and service (Wilke, Gmelch, and Lovrich 1985).

Stress, in proper amounts, is not bad. It is much like your body's temperature, in that you must have a certain level to stay alive. You are the doctor: Apply treatment only when faculty temperatures run above or below normal. The prescription is logical. In your department chair role of motivator, you must filter out excessive stress for some faculty and light fires under others to ignite their productivity. Review the following suggestions of techniques to remedy the situation of faculty suffering from lack of motivation (not enough stress) (Gmelch and Chan 1994).

Rust-Out Prevention Techniques

1. *Promote professional development.* Have faculty (a) participate in special workshops or seminars on new and effective teaching techniques, (b) brush up on the recent literature and research in their discipline by attending professional conferences, and (c) attend classes for professional and personal enrichment. In times of rapid change and advances in disciplines, faculty can become obsolete or outdated in their profession. Connect them with the numerous learned societies and professional associations available to them, so they can be periodically updated on the latest thinking in the field. If their jobs are as comfortable as an old shoe, they are not allowing for growth.

2. *Provide technical support.* Have you provided your faculty members with the tools necessary to do their job? Is every faculty member's office equipped with the latest in computer technology? In addition, make curriculum and reading materials available, such as McKeachie's *Teaching Tips* (1999), Weimer's *Improving Your Classroom Teaching* (1993), Thyer's *Suc-*

cessful Publishing in Scholarly Journals (1994), Seldin and Associates' *Improving College Teaching* (1995), Smelser's *Effective Committee Service* (1993), and Berger's *Improving Writing Skills* (1993). For encouragement and guidance, we provide every new department faculty member with a copy of *Getting Tenure* (Whicker, Kronenfeld, and Strickland 1993), Seldin's *The Teaching Portfolio* (1997), and Seldin and Higgerson's *The Administrative Portfolio* (2002). Consider other supportive materials as well, including the Jossey-Bass series on Academic Administrator's Guides and Davidson and Ambrose's *The New Professor's Handbook* (1994).

3. *Encourage innovation and risk taking.* Rather than punish faculty for taking risks, encourage them to experiment. As one management consultant commented, "If you are not making mistakes, you are not really trying." Invite faculty to be bold and to take risks to challenge their skills, but not so many that they are overwhelmed. Growth and productivity result when we take risks, so provide a safe environment for your faculty to do so without the fear of an occasional failure.

4. *Thrive on stress for success.* The most important avenue for faculty productivity is the crossroads where stress meets success. Search out new agendas for their teaching and writing. For example, encourage them to make writing a daily habit. Some faculty try to have at least three articles out under review at any given time. Challenge their teaching with new material and teaching methods. We once asked a premier consultant on effective teaching if he is as stressed now as he was when he first taught. His response: "No, but I am not as effective either."

5. *Develop associations and promote teamwork.* Often, faculty members' isolation magnifies their difficulties. Some have found that by joining collegial groups interested in teaching or specific areas of research, they can break their isolation and nurture a sense of peer support. On many campuses, faculty groups and centers on effective teaching and learning have formed and function as catalysts and support groups for those interested in honing their teaching skills. In the same vein, we have formed an interdisciplinary research group on stress and performance, out of which several national studies have emerged. Recently, the Center for the Study of Academic Leadership has been our salvation, keeping us active in our research while we maintain our full-time administrative positions. Some days, our most enjoyable and productive time is spent behind closed doors with our research teams.

6. *Change the scenery.* The simple act of changing courses, roles, or geography has been beneficial to many faculty. You, for example, may have even enjoyed the change in teaching assignments that came along with your department chair position. Faculty can also benefit from visiting other campuses, spending time with colleagues, taking sabbaticals, and participating in faculty exchange programs.

Burnout Prevention Techniques

At the other end of the stress and performance curve is burnout; as chair, you should be aware of the following techniques for helping faculty to avoid burnout.

1. *Have faculty break up their continuous assignments.* Although prevention suggests avoiding isolation, burnout results from the opposite—too many personal contacts taking up too much time and energy. Faculty suffer from what can be called encounter stress, from continuously dealing with people all day long. For them, the opposite provides relief—they may need to block periods of time in their day when they can close their doors and plan, write, or read without interruption.

2. *Help faculty understand the stress their jobs entail.* Do not let new faculty be caught off guard by the fact that their positions are loaded with stress. Let them know in advance that there are many stresses involved in research and teaching; that the demands are high, time insufficient, and performance expectations unrealistic. Help them to understand also that this stress can be the spice of faculty life, if they handle it correctly.

3. *Allow faculty to say no to extra opportunities when overloaded.* If you ask faculty members who already have full loads to take on extra activities, be sure you allow them to turn you down. Propose the extra activities as opportunities, not obligations.

4. *Break large projects into smaller parts.* The thought of teaching a three-credit course on a narrow subject for 45 hours over a semester is enough to burn anyone out before the semester even starts. The same is true of undertaking a major research project. Have faculty break large projects into smaller, more manageable parts and treat each separately, with its own time line and set of requirements.

5. *Help faculty find time for themselves, away from interruptions.* Experienced teachers often advocate the practice of blocking time for themselves, at least a few hours before class for preparation and reflection. One afternoon prior to class, one of the authors put a note on his door that read, "Please do not disturb—preparing for class." A couple of senior faculty later commented to him that it appeared he wasn't accessible. But do we have to be incessantly accessible, with perennially open doors? Won't classes be better if we are better prepared? The students respected that teaching was regarded as a high enough priority to warrant screened interruptions. With respect to our research, we have a separate project room, away from our administrative offices, to which we can retreat for research purposes.

6. *Help faculty pace themselves.* Faculty who effectively use stress for optimal performance often speak of their ability to pace themselves. Identify long-term tasks and the ones that will require additional resources of time and energy. Group the tasks to balance a set of high-demand tasks

with those requiring less rigor. For example, pace the number of new preparations or writing projects required. Give faculty the option of balancing their teaching, service, and research loads to minimize the number of new courses or projects in any given year or semester.

The strategies suggested here to prevent burnout and rust out can help faculty to either increase or decrease their stress. Finally, you should help faculty maintain and manage positive stress to obtain optimum performance. Each faculty member should be able to build a stable performance platform, with four sturdy legs to support it. The first of these legs is the establishment of a strong set of professional goals. The second leg is the taking of control over one's own destiny. The third is the building of a solid foundation of good health, fitness, and nutrition. The final leg is the ability to deal creatively with the conflict inherent in faculty life, in part by practicing the principles found in the works of Fisher and Ury, such as *Getting to Yes* (Fisher and Ury 1991) and *Getting Past No* (Ury 1993). Together, these four legs support a stable performance platform. If any of the legs is weak, fractured, or out of position, it affects the utility of the other three. All four legs must be strong and in place to support faculty performance.

MENTORING PROFESSIONAL DEVELOPMENT

Mentor programs typically are misunderstood or inappropriately labeled; they are generally neither well developed nor widely used. You should not accept total responsibility for coaching and mentoring all faculty in the department. Share this responsibility with competent and experienced members in your department. Although coaching and mentoring by senior faculty occur informally, you should establish designated mentors or mentor committees formally for each new faculty member.

Department chairs, for their part in the mentoring process, must provide the following guidance.

1. *Show concern for each faculty member's development.* Most chairs spend little time on career counseling with faculty. Faculty members are semiautonomous and have few rungs in their career ladders. The basic principle of mentoring is to show genuine concern for a person's personal development and career progress. The chair should establish with each faculty member an annual plan for his or her advancement (see Gmelch and Miskin 1993, chap. 6). Because most colleges and departments widely reward three basic categories of faculty performance—teaching, scholarship, and service—these three responsibilities should provide the basis for the annual plan. The plan could take the form of a professional portfolio (see Seldin 1997; Seldin and Higgerson 2002), a research agenda, or a set of service programs to be accomplished at the end of the year, not necessarily for annual review purposes but for self-development and advancement.

2. *Support program development opportunities.* Another way to promote skill development is to keep faculty informed about relevant workshop and seminar opportunities. The chair should encourage enrollment in workshops and seminars, and the department should cover the expenses. Some universities and colleges facilitate and encourage attendance not only by covering expenses but by providing financial compensation in the form of a daily stipend for attendance, or by rearranging faculty schedules to allow time away from daily duties.

3. *Provide special opportunities for skill development.* In addition to formal workshops, chairs and colleges can support the development of teaching and scholarship in other ways. One approach is to provide special projects and assignments. For example, allocating funds for summer research or teaching stipends to support research or innovative teaching techniques not only improves performance, but it elevates the visibility and importance of faculty.

4. *Promote faculty activities and accomplishments.* A department chair can promote the faculty reputation by making sure that students know about faculty members' achievements, expertise, and areas of interest. For example, a series of faculty colloquia can provide faculty the opportunity to share their interests and expertise. Special bulletins also can highlight faculty activities. Publish a monthly bulletin that highlights faculty activities in community service, partnerships, special teaching accomplishments, publications, and research interests. Not only do students and alumni appreciate knowing what faculty are doing, but our provost frequently writes notes to faculty members congratulating them on their accomplishments and activities. Eventually, the number of books published in our department one year caught the attention of the local newspaper, and it ended up as a front-page story. Clearly, someone is taking notice and providing recognition.

5. *Serve as a role model.* In our studies of department chairs, almost all chairs reported that they taught and maintained scholarship agendas while serving as chairs (Moses and Roe 1990; Gmelch, Carroll, et al. 1990, Gmelch, Burns, et al. 1992; Houchen and Gmelch 1994). This is your opportunity to demonstrate your prowess as a teacher and scholar. Invite others to join your scholarship team or to attend your classes. Offer your services as guest lecturer in their classes.

Networking with Colleagues

Through networking, faculty can develop and maintain contacts with other colleagues who possess important sources of information and assistance, both inside and outside the university setting. They can keep current with advances in their disciplines, become acquainted with groups of faculty members who have common interests, be introduced to influential individuals in their fields, and generally enhance their opportunities for professional advancement.

In your role as faculty developer, you need to help faculty members to set up both internal and external networks. Internal networking within the university or college, essential when there is high interdependence among departments and colleagues, is relatively easy. Department chairs are likely to have larger networks than do specialized faculty members, because the job requires chairs to transcend a myopic perspective and understand the university as a whole. Use your managerial networks to help faculty members connect with other scholars in your institution. Chairs can help get faculty involved in opportunities they normally may not be able to access.

In contrast, some ideas may be more acceptable to faculty if they come from their contacts in external networks—individuals in other universities, colleges, and professional associations, as well as client and customer groups—than if they come from internal sources. For example, three colleges at our university developed an interdisciplinary grant proposal to infuse total quality management (TQM) into our curriculum. The chairs from four disciplines were able to network faculty from different colleges to share and develop courses and team teach the principles of TQM. In addition, the deans of engineering and education have joined forces nationally to create a Deans' Summit to address common issues in technological literacy and innovative pedagogical practices (Gorham, Gmelch, et al. 2002).

Faculty members' rates of tenure and promotability may, in fact, be related to their ability to network effectively. As Boice (1992, 43) notes, faculty "cannot flourish in isolation. Before they will feel comfortable and efficient, they must find social supports and intellectual stimulation." This means relaxing the usual autonomy so often characteristic of faculty so that colleagues can assist each other in their teaching, service, and scholarship efforts. Boice found that "those new faculty who made teaching a collegial and sociable venture found the task of teaching easier and more rewarding" (80). The stark absence of collegial support and networking that exists in some institutions reinforces the need for chairs to facilitate faculty connectedness. Clearly, we need to find ways to change the culture of solitary faculty to a more public collectivity.

Networking Strategies

The following suggestions can help chairs use networking to support faculty development in their departments.

1. *Celebrate faculty excellence.* Use ceremonies, meetings, and social events to celebrate faculty successes (Thomas and Schuh 2004). Talk with faculty, even informally, before, during, and after these events about the importance of their teaching and scholarship. Once, at an Australian uni-

versity, the first author was visiting a colleague who had just published a book. The colleague's department chair had organized a "book launch"—a ceremonial event during which colleagues join together to throw a party and present testimonials to the newly published author's scholarship. Given the delightful Aussie humor, these events can get a bit raucous, but that only adds to the flavor of the tales, the cultural history of the department, and the connectedness of the colleagues.

2. *Provide opportunities for faculty members to form interest groups.* If you know the specific interests of your faculty members, you can form groups to introduce your colleagues to others interested in similar research, service projects, or teaching opportunities. When the first author was a new faculty member at the University of Oregon, a senior professor asked three of the new "bright-eyed, bushy-tailed" assistant professors from three different disciplines to join him for lunch on Mondays to discuss a common scholarship interest, stress. One colleague was a sport psychologist, another was a teacher educator, and the third (the first author) was a managerial behavioral scientist. The group referred to themselves as the Monday Lunch Bunch. Now, 30 years later, the Lunch Bunch members are all full professors, they work in three different regions of the country, but they still keep in contact—thanks to the initiative of a supportive senior faculty member (Robert Sylwester, now retired but still in contact by mail and an occasional crossing at professional meetings).

3. *Be accessible to provide social support.* Not all faculty members feel comfortable scheduling appointments with an administrator to talk off the record about troubles they may be having. Chairs need to build in flexibility so that they have time simply to "wander" the halls, to be accessible to faculty. Although this may not appear to be the most efficient use of your time, you will find that it can pay dividends in heading off problems before they have a chance to grow. The first author once offered formally to block time each Monday to work with a new faculty member on some teaching difficulties he was having. Although the faculty member appreciated this gesture, he asked if the chair couldn't just informally stop by his office and chat—be his colleague, his friend. From his informal chats with this faculty member, the author understood more about his problem and was able to put him in contact with some of the faculty stars who could give him some tips on his teaching; thus, he was able to get the help he needed without feeling he had to disclose his weaknesses to the department chair. As much as a chair may want to be a colleague first, in the eyes of new faculty he or she still represents the ultimate evaluator for tenure and promotion.

4. *Be discreet about faculty problems.* Learn to be empathetic and understanding when someone is anxious or upset about his or her performance (Gmelch 1996b, 1998). When a problem comes to your attention, find a discreet way to give support. Many activities and information, such

as your department's budget, should be public knowledge, but not the private conversations you have in confidence with troubled faculty members.

5. *Facilitate faculty members' opportunities to join formal groups.* Most department chairs have had, on the average, 18 years of experience in their disciplines before becoming academic administrators (Carroll 1991). Over those years, you probably have developed a wealth of external contacts and knowledge of professional opportunities. Set faculty up with these external networks, such as professional associations, learned societies, and even workshops. You may even be in a position to nominate a colleague to serve as a proposal reviewer, an editorial board member, or an association officer. Use your contacts to get your faculty members connected.

6. *Keep in contact with network members.* When you attend professional meetings, use the opportunity to make new contacts and renew old ones. Take advantage of today's technology, and set up your network on e-mail. After taking part in a National Kellogg Fellowship and Harvard's Management Development Program, fellow participants are "hooked up" for life. As the saying goes, there are no "former" fellows—once a fellow, always a fellow. Introduce your faculty to the importance of network contacts, and help them get started.

Now, Select from the Menu

As we have noted, the most important role of department chairs is the development of faculty. In this chapter we have reviewed some of the behaviors you need to exhibit to support the development of your faculty. While working with faculty, recall the four supportive behaviors we have discussed—modeling, motivating, mentoring, and networking. However, you may not easily recall the specific strategies we have suggested. They represent a smorgasbord of ideas from which you should pick and practice as appropriate. To aid you in the recollection and selection of these strategies, we list them again here in the form of a sort of menu you can use when searching for ways to nurture your faculty.

Modeling
- Have faculty:
  observe others teaching,
  join research groups,
  get involved in community projects, and
  search for tips of the trade.

Motivating
- Recognize the positive and negative relationships between stress and faculty performance.

- Prevent faculty rust-out by:

    promoting professional development,
    providing technical support,
    encouraging innovation and risk taking,
    thriving on stress for success,
    developing associations and promoting teamwork, and
    changing the scenery.

- Reduce faculty burnout by:

    having faculty break up their continuous assignments,
    helping faculty be aware of the stress their job entails,
    allowing faculty to say no to extra opportunities,
    breaking large   projects into smaller parts,
    helping faculty find time for themselves, and
    helping faculty pace themselves.

Mentoring

- Show concern for each faculty member's development.
- Support program-development opportunities.
- Provide special opportunities for skill development.
- Promote faculty activities and accomplishments.
- Serve as a role model.

Networking

- Celebrate faculty excellence.
- Provide opportunities to form interest groups.
- Be accessible to provide social support.
- Be discreet about faculty problems.
- Facilitate faculty opportunities to join formal groups.
- Keep in contact with network members.

Chapter 4

MOTIVATE FACULTY PERFORMANCE

— Your Only Choice —

> The real challenge of a good manager is
> not to find superior people but to motivate
> ordinary people to do superior work.
> —Richard Rybolt

Supporting faculty activities is only half of the coin of nurturing successful faculty members in your department. You must be proactive, finding ways to motivate your faculty by reinforcing effective practices, evaluating results, recognizing and rewarding accomplishments, and ultimately promoting faculty based on their successes. As Table 1.2 in chapter 1 shows, 85 to 89 percent of department chairs feel that among their most important tasks are the encouragement of faculty research and publications and the professional development of faculty. Therefore, this chapter should be meaningful to you in your efforts to develop a productive department.

How does the chair know what to advocate? Faculty basically have three fiduciary responsibilities: teaching, scholarship, and service. Most promotion and tenure committees make their decisions based on the "big three." Some departments may add another factor or two because of special circumstances or historical impediments. For example, one department added a factor called "interpersonal relationship," or citizenship, because one junior faculty member had met all three basic requirements, but he was such an incorrigible colleague that no one wanted him around. As department chair, make sure you advocate for your faculty such that they have balanced all criteria into a portfolio of productivity.

All three goals of effective teaching, scholarly productivity, and community service are ambiguous to some extent. Recent scholars and faculty handbooks at some universities have changed faculty responsibilities to learning, discovery, and engagement (Boyer 1990; Glassick, Huber, and Maeroff 1997). Some consider scholarly productivity and community service to be easier to track and evaluate than teaching, but recently, even "hard-copy" scholarly publications are up for reconsideration as to what constitutes scholarship (see Boyer 1990).

Our aim in this chapter is not to engage in an academic debate on the precise benchmarks of faculty productivity. More guidelines are provided in chapter 6. However, for the sake of discussion, what should you advocate in the area of teaching? Researchers have led us to five overlapping and interrelated components that make up effective teaching:

1. Enthusiasm

2. Preparation and organization

3. Ability to stimulate student thought and interest

4. Clarity

5. Knowledge and love of the content

Without elaboration, this brief listing should be clear to most faculty. They should also have a sense of what it takes to be an effective faculty member, but sometimes they do not. Your job as chair is first to clarify and then reinforce their performance in these areas. "A good teacher entails more than a decision to be enthusiastic, organized, clear, stimulating, and knowledgeable. It involves translating those abstract ingredients into tangible behaviors, policies, and practices" (Weimer 1993, 16).

REINFORCING PERFORMANCE

How can you as chair reinforce effective service, scholarship, and learning in your department? Where do you start? On the whole, you can assume that most faculty perform admirably. However, some have not maximized their capabilities. As one college president, and now American Association for Higher Education president, testified, "Most members of the professoriate are dedicated scholars and teachers. . . . But for many of them the fun seems to have gone out of their work" (Lovett 1993, 3). Many faculty can improve without outside help, but others need an advocate to support and reinforce their activities.

Is there a particular method you can use to reinforce faculty performance? In a study of effective chairs, Creswell and his colleagues (1990) suggest the following five-step process.

Step 1: Gather background information. Before approaching a faculty member about performance problems, gather data about his or her activities, beyond the formal student evaluations, published manuscripts, and committee service. Consider the multiple sources. For instance, visit with students, talk with senior faculty, and tap into the grapevine—staff, students, faculty, and other administrators. Your support staff may have the most reliable information from their contact with faculty, students, and their own perceptions of work submitted to them. Take notes from all these sources and look for reliability and validity among the data you have collected.

Step 2: Meet with the faculty member to clarify the problem, then set goals and objectives. After you have gathered your information, schedule a meeting with the faculty member at a mutually convenient time and neutral location. At this point, describe the problematic behaviors or actions that have come to your attention. Do not use evaluative words; rather, keep to objective descriptions and ask for the faculty member's perception of the same situation. When both of you agree on the problem, then explore possible ways to rectify the situation. Set some goals and positive courses of action. At this juncture, it may be wise to summarize your meeting with a memo outlining the situation and the steps that will be taken. Ask the faculty member how you can be of assistance, and explain that your role is to reinforce his or her success, not to dwell on any failure. The million-dollar decision to hire this faculty member has already been made. The bottom line is evident: It costs more to have a faculty member fail, and be relieved of his or her duties, than to put in the time and energy to make that person succeed.

Step 3: Observe the performance yourself. Although the principle of faculty autonomy usually means that faculty have the right to teach behind closed doors, most faculty manuals and administrative policies provide chairs with both the right and the responsibility to observe faculty members' teaching performance directly. Your objective with a troubled faculty member is to explore the potential problem so that appropriate improvement can be developed. In cases where you feel direct observation by the department chair may be too threatening, you can ask a senior faculty mentor to observe classroom instruction, review manuscripts, or evaluate contributions made to committees and formally report back directly to the faculty member and chair. This worked very effectively in a case involving the first author and one of his branch campus faculty members who was teaching in a discipline out of the author's area of expertise. Because the author's observation of teaching could have been seen as evaluative and for administrative purposes, he requested that a senior faculty mentor observe the other faculty member's teaching for the explicit purpose of improvement.

Step 4: Facilitate improvement and the practice of new skills. You and/or the faculty mentor may need to help the faculty member develop a plan for improvement. With regard to teaching, you may refer the faculty member to books on teaching, provide him or her with strategies that have worked for you, or offer him or her the opportunity to attend workshops or to observe some of your best faculty teaching. With regard to scholarship, you may have to set up some early benchmarks as reasonable indicators of progress. For example, if publications are desirable and rewarded, get the faculty member to develop an area of interest, draft a proposed manuscript, join another faculty member publishing in the area, or take part in other activities that will ultimately lead to successful publication.

Step 5: Monitor the progress of and encourage faculty productivity. Revert to Step 1 and gather new information on the progress being achieved by the faculty member. It may take time to see results, but you have a moral obligation to your colleagues and an ethical commitment to your institution to try to help struggling faculty improve their performance. You cannot wait until the third-year review, or even annual review, to detect difficulties and provide feedback for improvement.

EVALUATING RESULTS

Reinforcing activities should occur throughout the year. Annually, however, most chairs are obliged to undertake a formal evaluation of each faculty member's research, teaching, and service productivity. A dean and a leading scholar in faculty assessment shed some light on evaluation in academe:

> The credibility of faculty assessment remains one of the most precarious and sensitive issues on campus. . . . Research productivity is considered the easiest and most fairly measured. Because evaluation of teaching effectiveness is often based solely on student ratings, it is seen as a mere popularity contest. Finally, the quality of professional service activities is seen to be rarely judged at all. (Braskamp and Ory 1994, 5)

Clearly, evaluating one's colleagues represents the chair's most reprehensible responsibility, but it is also the most important. As disclosed in Table 1.2, 9 out of 10 department chairs believe that evaluating faculty performance is a critically important task. Ironically, the same group of chairs recognizes faculty evaluation as the task for which they are in greatest need of training (see Table 1.3).

The process of faculty evaluation represents a book in itself. Several helpful volumes have been written, including Seldin's *The Teaching Portfolio* (1997) and *Changing Practices in Faculty Evaluation* (1994), Braskamp and Ory's *Assessing Faculty Work* (1994), and Centra's *Reflective Faculty Evaluation* (1993). For the finer points in validity and reliability of faculty evaluation practices, consult these resources. For now, as department chair, you have three basic questions to answer: (1) What are you going to evaluate? (2) For what purpose(s) are you evaluating faculty? and (3) What system will you use to evaluate faculty?

What Should You Evaluate?

Most universities and colleges cite teaching, research, and service as the central academic functions of faculty, although the amount of importance assigned to each varies from institution to institution. In fact, many institutions assess scholarship rather than research and value community interaction over publications.

Besides the traditional three categories of faculty work, we suggest a fourth: citizenship. Although being a good citizen may be assumed, we place it in a separate category to emphasize its significance in the building of a productive department. Good citizenship is not only desired but necessary for a productive community of scholars. You may have noticed that in the sample job advertisement in chapter 2 (Exhibit 2.1), teamwork and the ability to build collaborative relationships are specified in the section on job qualifications.

The exact work that faculty perform in each of the four categories is difficult to describe, define, or delimit. Faculty manuals provide some guidance, but not to the satisfaction of most chairs and faculty. Therefore, the faculty evaluation process should begin with clarification and agreement as to the faculty member's duties within each of the four areas of responsibility. A sample list of such duties follows; others can be found in books such as *Assessing Faculty Work,* by Braskamp and Ory (1994).

- Teaching
  Instructing
  Advising and supervising students
  Developing instructional skills and strategies
- Research and Creative Work
  Publishing manuscripts
  Conducting research
  Creating community programs
  Applying scholarly works in the field
  Seeking funding for research activities
- Service
  Providing consultative services to clientele
  Serving on university, college, and department committees
  Serving professional societies and associations

> Providing leadership in one's discipline and educational community
- Citizenship
> Mentoring new faculty members
> Promoting and supporting colleagues
> Accepting responsibility for major projects and causes
> Contributing to the enhancement of department teamwork and collaboration

Specific performance measures for these and other faculty duties can be found in the section on action planning in chapter 7.

Why Evaluate Faculty?

Faculty evaluation can serve many purposes; for example, evaluation results can be used to improve performance, to reward performance, to supply information for administrative decision making, to supply information for customers, to protect the individual, to protect the organization, to provide a basis for individual development and growth, to aid in the selection of individuals, and to provide a basis for promotion and tenure.

Given the possible array of purposes, you as department chair must make some choices, for unless and until you find out specifically what you want to know and why you want to know it, faculty evaluation is likely to be mired in conflicting expectations. This becomes readily apparent when, upon further inspection of the comparative purposes of faculty evaluation, we find that some purposes are in conflict, some overlap, some differ with respect to objectives and goals, and some vary according to their institutional settings (see Table 4.1). The multiple purposes also require different kinds of data, from different sources, at different times, and using different designs. In sum, the all-purpose evaluation may be a myth (Gmelch and Glasman 1976).

The five-step process given previously for reinforcing faculty performance also fills the requirements of evaluation for the purpose of faculty self-improvement. As reflected in Table 4.1, evaluation intended to aid self-improvement primarily looks at detailed information in a non-comparative, collaborative, diagnostic manner at continuous times throughout the year. In contrast, evaluation for administrative decision-making purposes is more judgmental in nature, using summary, semicomparative data, and is conducted at the end of a certain time period, whether it be annual or at the end of a three-year term. These qualities characterize a promotion and tenure evaluation system—for the purpose of administrative decision making.

What you need to do is pull together and organize information on how to conduct faculty evaluations so that "individual improvement and insti-

Table 4.1. Data Requirements of Faculty Evaluation: Dimensions and Purposes

DIMENSIONS	PURPOSES		
	Self-improvement	Administrative decision making	Client information
	(To acquire and diagnose information to improve oneself)	(To provide an information base for personnel decisions)	(To provide evaluative information for enlightened consumption)
Nature of data	diagnostic	judgmental	descriptive
Level of specificity	detailed	summary	summary
Method of reporting	noncomparative	semicomparative	comparative
Timing	continuous	end of term	end of term
Audience	self	faculty and administrators	clients

tutional accountability, as two ends of a continuum, will come together" (Braskamp and Ory 1994, 11). Clearly, you should build, to the greatest extent possible, a process that provides both you and the faculty member with information for purposes of faculty improvement and administrative decision making.

How Should Faculty Be Evaluated?

How can you blend both the requirements and qualities of self-improvement with administrative decision making into a fair and equitable evaluation process for faculty? The management by objectives (MBO) process, which has been around since the late 1940s and was popularized in the 1960s in the corporate world, has the qualities needed to solicit faculty input into the evaluation process and to ensure objectivity for promotion and tenure decisions. In chapter 7, we provide a modified MBO system that we call the *faculty action plan,* which promotes objective evaluation, linked to department goals, but with a focus on faculty development.

You should strive to develop an evaluation plan that will keep you and your faculty on target while blending in individual improvement and institutional accountability. Iowa State University's faculty senate has adopted Position Responsibility Statements (PRS) for each faculty member to specify the percentage of time they devote to each of their major responsibilities (i.e., teaching and learning, 40 percent; scholarship, 40 percent; and service/ engagement, 20 percent). No matter what plan you adopt, it should include at least the following four key steps.

Step 1: Outline key activities within each of the faculty responsibilities. As a starting point, check the ones suggested under this section's first question: What should you evaluate?

Step 2: Gain agreement on the objectives targeted for the next academic year. For example, in the area of teaching, the faculty member may indicate that his or her objective is to teach, successfully, three classes each semester; in the area of advising, the faculty member could indicate the number of his or her students who will graduate, the number of undergraduate advisees he or she will oversee, and so on.

Step 3: Develop indicators of success for each of the objectives. Just as in golf, you and your faculty need to know what is par for the course. Steps taken toward accomplishing objectives should also be published on a scorecard. You can use something like the action planning form shown in Figure 7.1 in chapter 7 to list the measures of successful completion of objectives. For illustrative purposes, in chapter 7 we suggest possible measures to consider in each of the faculty areas of responsibility.

Step 4: Establish a periodic feedback system with faculty members to check progress. Have faculty indicate the dates and results they expect. Without specific deadlines and continuous effort, some activities may be unrealistically postponed and never get done. For example, the junior faculty member who says he or she will wait until summer to engage in research may not realize that some activities do not just happen all at once but take constant care and attention. Regarding senior faculty, many universities and colleges have instituted post-tenure review processes.

If you make the evaluation a truly collaborative process in which you ask faculty to set their own objectives and time lines, you will not only advocate the success of your faculty, but you will efficiently budget your department resources as well (see chapter 6).

RECOGNIZING ACCOMPLISHMENTS

Recognition of faculty successes can come in many forms, but most common are praise and awards. Neither has to cost your department fiscal resources; you simply have to catch faculty members doing things right and reward them with verbal commendations, expressions of appreciation, or other gestures that acknowledge their accomplishments. You need to be out and about to find out who is achieving success. When you find a faculty member who is doing things right, comment on the spot and follow up with a letter of commendation for his or her file (with a copy to the dean). Eventually, you may wish to nominate the individual for a faculty excellence award.

Recognition for faculty excellence has traditionally been viewed as taking the form of monetary rewards, but numerous other mechanisms present powerful alternatives to financial benefits. Most praise is private, but praise can be used in public rituals, exhibitions, and ceremonies as well. You can publicize faculty accomplishments through news releases or on department bulletin boards displaying acts of scholarship, service, and teaching. Yearly faculty excellence awards can be bestowed at the department level to help ensure a motivating environment to support faculty excellence.

Remember, formal awards symbolically communicate the chair's values and priorities. A recognition ceremony at commencement or special ceremony, for example, ensures that faculty achievements are acknowledged not only by the department chair but by others in the college. The honoring of faculty also sends a strong symbolic message to those in the audience—your clientele and their friends and families.

Decisions concerning faculty recognition should be based on the following questions: What should be recognized? When should recognition be given? Who should be recognized? What form of recognition should be used? Given these questions, the following guidelines may be helpful:

- Recognize a variety of faculty contributions and achievements: teaching, research, service, and citizenship.
- Actively search for faculty contributions to recognize.
- Recognize improvements in faculty performance.
- Recognize commendable faculty efforts that may have failed.
- Do not limit recognition to senior faculty—boost the morale of new and junior faculty as well.
- Do not limit recognition only to your few best faculty members, because others may feel that recognition is not within their reach.
- Provide specific recognition for unique achievements, such as innovative teaching techniques, submission of grant proposals, and provision of service to the field.
- Provide timely recognition—once-a-year rituals alone will not motivate the masses.
- Use an appropriate form of recognition that is accepted by faculty members.

REWARDING ACHIEVEMENTS

Rewards are different from recognition in that they involve tangible benefits for effective performance, significant achievement, or assistance provided to faculty members or teaching assistants. Rewards may take the form of merit increases, promotions, or better job assignments.

One national study of faculty stress found that lack of rewards and recognition accounted for most of the stress experienced by faculty (Gmelch, Wilke, and Lovrich 1986). The stressors identified by faculty include inadequate rewards, insufficient recognition, and unclear expectations in all three areas of faculty responsibility: teaching, research, and service (Gmelch, Lovrich, and Wilke 1984).

With respect to insufficient and unclear rewards, department chairs can undertake goal-setting sessions such as are used in the MBO process discussed earlier in this chapter. At a minimum, you should establish an annual meeting to address rewarded activities for the year in teaching, research, service, and citizenship. You can also introduce a more comprehensive portfolio concept encompassing all four areas of responsibility, such that faculty members who are already tenured may not be expected to produce excellence in all four areas every year, but possibly excellence in one and competence in the other three. In this way, the established objectives can be discussed in relation to their congruence with department priorities such that each individual faculty member, when combined with the faculty as a whole, represents a department productivity portfolio. Each is then rewarded for his or her contribution to the department portfolio.

The opportunities for rewarding faculty may be limited on two accounts. First, chairs may not have the resources to dispense many tangible rewards, such as merit-pay increases. Second, chairs may not have the authority to give rewards because faculty excellence awards are usually governed by faculty committees, formal policies, and reward systems at the college or university level. But you should not miss opportunities to nominate and promote your colleagues. Even if you have limited reward power, the following guidelines may help you to find ways to reward faculty achievements:

- Find out what rewards are attractive to faculty.
- Find out what rewards are available both within and outside your institution.
- Identify and evaluate the relevant aspects of faculty performance to be rewarded.
- Explain the criteria used to determine rewards.
- Distribute rewards in a fair way.
- Give rewards in a timely manner.

A Road Map for Faculty Motivation

In this chapter we have provided you with some steps and ideas on how to reinforce the performance of faculty members, evaluate their results, recognize their accomplishments, and reward their achievements. These steps and ideas constitute a road map you can use to help faculty members head in the direction of tenure, promotion, and professional advancement. To aid you in the recollection and selection of these strategies, we present the road map for you again here in outline form:

- Five Steps to Reinforce Faculty Performance
  1. Gather background data.
  2. Meet to clarify problems; then set goals and objectives.
  3. Observe performance yourself.
  4. Facilitate improvement and the practice of new skills.
  5. Monitor progress and advocate for the faculty member.
- Basic Questions to Answer in Evaluating Faculty
  1. What should you evaluate?
  2. Why should you evaluate faculty?
  3. How should you evaluate faculty?

  Step 1: Outline key activities within faculty responsibilities.

  Step 2: Gain agreement on targeted objectives for the academic year.

  Step 3: Develop indicators of success for objectives.

  Step 4: Establish a periodic feedback system to check progress.
- Guidelines for Recognizing Faculty

  Recognize a variety of achievements.

  Actively search for contributions.

  Recognize performance improvements.

  Recognize new and junior faculty.

  Do not limit recognitions to the few best.

  Recognize unique achievements.

  Provide timely recognition.

  Use appropriate forms of recognition.
- Guidelines for Rewarding Faculty

  Identify attractive rewards.

  Search for rewards within and outside your institution.

  Reward relevant aspects of faculty performance.

  Explain criteria used to determine rewards.

  Distribute rewards in a fair way.

  Give rewards in a timely manner.

PROMOTING FACULTY SUCCESS

The ultimate rewards for faculty come in the forms of tenure and promotion. If you take seriously the supporting and motivating behaviors discussed in this chapter, and if you perform them effectively, you should find the challenge of promoting your faculty into rank or tenure to be easy. This is where your million-dollar decision pays off. If your faculty-development system is successful, you should have modeled productive faculty behaviors, motivated faculty with positive stress and challenges, mentored faculty to behave in productive ways, networked faculty with successful and supportive colleagues, reinforced faculty for appropriate activities and actions, evaluated faculty results to provide timely feedback, recognized faculty for their everyday accomplishments, and rewarded faculty for their achievements.

Even your excellent untenured faculty members will have feelings of insecurity and uncertainty, so be sure to provide them with the moral support they may need. Now is the time to promote them for all they have achieved and encourage and support their continued growth throughout their professional careers.

Several guides are available to assist you and your faculty in the quest for tenure and promotion. The Survival Skills for Scholars series includes a volume titled *Getting Tenure* (Whicker, Kronefeld, and Strickland 1993). This handbook starts with words of wisdom on the subjective political process and concludes with three important chapters on meeting the objective criterion in research, teaching, and service. Other resources published for new faculty include Robert Boice's *The New Faculty Member* (1992), Gerald Gibson's *Good Start: A Guidebook for New Faculty in Liberal Arts Colleges* (1992), Cliff Davidson and Susan Ambrose's *The New Professor's Handbook* (1994), David Johnson and colleagues' *Active Learning: Cooperation in the College Classroom* (Johnson, Johnson, and Smith 1998), and William McKeachie's *Teaching Tips* (1999). Consider these resources as you explore your manager and leader roles in chapters 5, 6, and 7.

PART II

MANAGER

Chapter 5

CHAIR AS MANAGER

— Budgeting Sets the Stage —

Business is never so healthy as when, like
a chicken, it must do a certain amount
of scratching for what it gets.
—Henry Ford

Meetings, schedules, facilities, curricula, enrollments, budgets. Sound familiar? These are responsibilities most department chairs do not enjoy. This managing role is the fiduciary responsibility referred to in chapter 1. Even the most academic of your department activities must be adequately supported. Most chairs in our study cited resource management as critical to their success and asserted that resource difficulties are the root of most staff and faculty dissatisfactions. Recall that the survey results displayed in Table 1.2 show both the management of department resources and the preparation and proposal of budgets to be among the 12 most important tasks of department chairs. Interestingly, the same chairs reported resource planning and budgeting to be among the top 12 areas in which they feel the need for additional training (Table 1.3). Effective management of department resources (gaining access to and allocation of those resources) may not be fun, but it is fundamental to your other department chair roles.

BEGIN WITH BUDGETS

Department budgets are not managed in isolation. You must share information openly and interact regularly with other administrators and with faculty in order to provide the resources to sustain your faculty productivity and encourage individual achievements that will accomplish your important department outcomes (resource sufficiency).

You may have heard the budgeting process at your institution described as "an economic prediction," "a political activity," "an organizational plan," or even as "the true management control process." However, among these varying concepts, universal agreement seems to appear—the tendency to view budgets as constraints on department activity. Thus a budget is typically defined as a plan or schedule for a certain period of time that limits and adjusts expenses to match an estimated, but fixed, amount of money allocated for that period. For example, if a department with 24 faculty members has a budget of $48,000 in annual teaching support, the chair may see the challenge as how to spread that amount evenly throughout the year ($4,000 per month) or how to divide it equally among faculty ($2,000 per faculty member). This usually results in inadequate support for some projects and tends to make all faculty members a little bit unhappy. It focuses management decisions on the false premise that you must reduce, restrict, or limit all department spending.

In reality, your management challenge is to determine the accomplishments that define success for your department and then find ways to fund those activities at sufficient levels. The activities of some faculty members may need to be restricted temporarily so that others may receive support for particularly important projects. Or special attention might be directed toward finding additional dollars for specific projects. In any event, managing budgets requires you to set priorities and make difficult allocation and reallocation decisions. But it does not mean you need to reduce allocations for all department activities. In this chapter, we explore the key issues underlying your search for department resources and your role in setting priorities for the academic budget; then, in chapter 6, we examine your implementation of this process and the critical issues of budget communications.

Budget Perspectives

Let's face it, managing department resources requires your active participation in the budget process. The academic budget process, whether in public or private schools, is a series of resource request and allocation decisions that distribute resources to the various parts of the organization. As in the circulatory system in the human body, it is the flow of blood (budgets) that supports the bodily functions (academic activities). At least in the short run, the body manages its blood supply by increasing the heart rate as needed (budget timing) and by enlarging or constricting selected arteries and vessels (budget priorities).

Many argue that allocation decisions are social or political in nature, based on existing power structures and negotiation strategies; that is, perhaps it is not the organs that need the blood the most that get the supply, but those that have the best access. Others suggest that these decisions are made on the basis of objective criteria, measurable goals, and organization outcomes; that is, blood flows to those parts of the body that are in most need of the blood supply. These two views are typically expressed in the political and rational budget models in higher education (Tucker 1992). We review these two budget models here, not to evaluate the models but to gain insight into your responsibilities for managing department resources.

Political Models

The political budgeting model considers primarily the social and human values in an organization (Volk, Slaughter, and Thomas 2001). It emphasizes the power structures and negotiation strategies involved. Rather than efficiency and economy, this model suggests, budget decisions rely more on administrative skills in bargaining, advocating, compromising, and negotiating.

The politics of budgeting typically rely on expense data in relation to previous budget periods and to other academic units. The "incremental budgeting approach" begins with the previous year's expenses and then states all budget requests as increases or increments in relation to this base. For instance, your decisions may be based on how much you can afford to add to last year's faculty travel budget, rather than on what each faculty member's travel will accomplish this year. The comparative budget format shows line items as a percentage of similar line items in other budgeting units (competing disciplines, other schools, similar programs in other states, and so on). The incremental process operates from the base of previous budget agreements and requires only budget item increases to be negotiated. The comparative or formula-based system selects comparative ratios that best represent the interests of the institution. In either case, both external and internal comparisons play a larger part in the budgeting process. As other units are perceived as more effective, or as external conditions worsen, your budget requests become less likely to be approved. The political budgeting model attends to overall budget changes and differences rather than linking budgets to the achievement of specific goals and objectives.

Rational Models

In contrast to the political model, the rational model is based on the theory of economic rationality and proposes that objectives and goals drive all organizational activity (Priem and Butler 2001). Rensis Likert (1961) introduced the managerial "link-pin" theory that the plans and goals of all subunits should combine to contribute collectively to the overall goals of the organization. With this in mind as you turn in your budget requests, you can improve your access to budget dollars if you can show how you are assisting in accomplishing the broader college and institutional goals. Whether you use a planning, programming, and budgeting system (PPBS) or a more general goal-oriented model, there is an advantage to making your budget requests on the basis of specific annual goals. Directing additional funds toward one faculty member's development of an interactive program between students and potential employers will surely have a more favorable impact on the future than will making sure that all faculty are treated exactly the same regardless of their plans.

You might expect political budgeting activities to become more prevalent during conditions of scarce resources, but research shows that political budgeting increases in the absence of objective criteria, rather than as a result of scarce resources. Political models tend to emphasize the overall budgets, while rational models focus on specific areas, outcomes, and measures. The political models rely on information and opinion of internal and external stakeholders rather than the programs and faculty successes measured in the rational models. Table 5.1 offers a more detailed comparison of the measures that the two budget models tend to emphasize. You may find this comparison useful as you consider your management role in the budget process.

As department chair, your interest is not in which approach is most accurate or which methods are currently most accepted but in understanding that both organizational goals and organizational politics are always part of the process. It is not that one set of measures is more or less important, but that they are different. There is value in the advice to "set your priorities to guide your budget allocations" and "allocate your budgets to encourage your faculty and department priorities." It is true that you can best manage effectively those activities that can be linked (operationally) to your desired department results.

The academic planning and budgeting process takes place over an extended period of time, but resource decisions (the blood flow) are necessary to give emphasis and life to your faculty efforts and program successes (bodily functions). Just as the medical doctor must understand the biological system of the human body to manage your health, you can improve your effectiveness as department chair by managing your department priorities through the budget requests and allocation decisions.

MANAGE YOUR DEPARTMENT

Whatever else the budget process in your institution accomplishes, it should encourage you to consciously set priorities. Whether intentional or not, priorities are established as budget allocations are made. Sufficient resources are seldom available to support every faculty request, to undertake

Table 5.1. Political and Rational Budget Models: Comparison of Typical Measures

POLITICAL EMPHASIS	RATIONAL EMPHASIS
All department expense items as a percentage of college expense items	Quantifiable accreditation standards
	Specific contract requirements
All department expense items as a percentage of institution expense items	Direct-contact teaching hours
	Reported teaching preparation hours
	Research presentations and publications
All department expense items in relation to all other departments within the institution	Reported service hours
	Professional development hours
All department expense items in relation to similar departments in other institutions	Enrollment numbers and trends
	Faculty and student ratios
	Faculty positions and promotions
Expense trends over time (current year in relation to previous years)	Research quantity and quality measures
	Extramural grants and contracts
Allocations in relation to economic trends	Program acceptance
Allocations in relation to college and institutional budgets	Student completion and placement rates
	Diversity issues
Allocations in relation to state and federal funding	Staffing levels
	Faculty turnover measures
Allocations in relation to external stakeholder support	Faculty development requirements
	Enrollment trends
Allocations in relation to institution, college, and department sponsors	Program majors
	Program expenditures
Perceived subunit strengths (organizational power)	Accreditation requirements
Negotiation skills and strategies	Service hours

SOURCE: Information for this table comes from the following works: Barney and Arikan (2001), Cameron (1983), Chaffee (1983), Gonyea (1980), Grobmyer, (2002), Hackman (1985), Layzell (1996), Makadok (2001), Orwig and Caruthers (1980), Rubin (1980), Schick (1985), Schmidtlein (1990), Tucker (1992), Vandament (1989), Volk, Slaughter, and Thomas (2001), and Waggaman (1991). These references are excellent sources for more detailed data on academic budget models.

every desired department activity, or to fund all colleges at the highest levels. At all budget levels, some requests will be funded and some will be denied or deferred. The act of making resource allocation decisions, either directly or indirectly, sets priorities. Whether you make them with conscious intent to encourage faculty productivity and goals or for more general or political reasons, your budget decisions give direction and focus to your faculty and staff activities.

Although the specific budget decisions in private colleges may differ from those in public institutions, both processes will include at least five levels of administrative participation (see Figure 5.1):

Figure 5.1. The Resource Request-Allocation Relationship

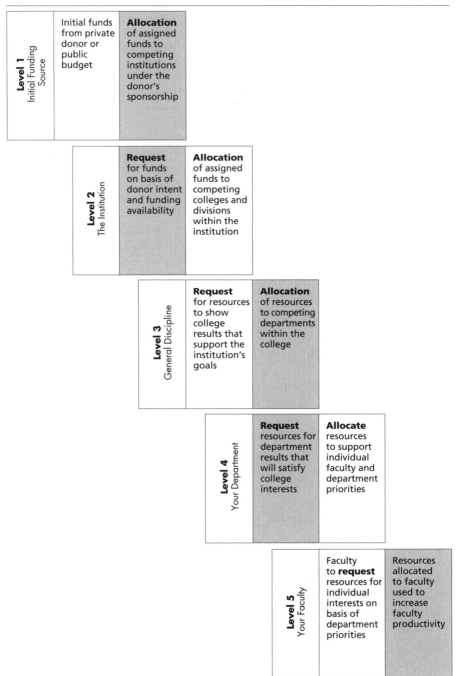

Level 1
Initial Funding Source

Initial funds from private donor or public budget

Allocation of assigned funds to competing institutions under the donor's sponsorship

Level 2
The Institution

Request for funds on basis of donor intent and funding availability

Allocation of assigned funds to competing colleges and divisions within the institution

Level 3
General Discipline

Request for resources to show college results that support the institution's goals

Allocation of resources to competing departments within the college

Level 4
Your Department

Request resources for department results that will satisfy college interests

Allocate resources to support individual faculty and department priorities

Level 5
Your Faculty

Faculty to **request** resources for individual interests on basis of department priorities

Resources allocated to faculty used to increase faculty productivity

1. Initial funding source (private sponsors/state and federal agencies)
2. Institutional level (universities/colleges)
3. General discipline level (schools/colleges/divisions)
4. Operational level (departments/programs/centers)
5. Individual level (faculty and staff)

The Initial Funding Source

In private institutions, the long-term endowment base, like the general health of the body, is a sign of overall (financial) well-being. However, continuing gifts, student tuitions, and the level of development activities, like the biological nutrients required to enrich the blood supply, have impacts on the quality and availability of future resources. In publicly funded schools, the process at this initial level may frequently be more complex and uncertain. Public allocations are based not only on the goals and priorities of the institution but in large part on the status of the economy, specialized legislative interests, and the priority of higher education in the public eye.

You may not be directly involved with your institution's initial funding level, but you will want to keep informed of its current status as you develop your department budget. It is important for you to know whether the existing public system is stressed or if the financial health of the private system is deteriorating or shifting. Although you may not be able to initiate changes at this level, you certainly need to be aware of such conditions.

Institutional-Level Budgets (University)

Private institutions are often guided by clearly mandated directives from their endowment funds, whereas public institutions are typically forced to struggle with the changing interests of taxpayers and legislators. In both cases, institutions must make their best efforts to clarify how they will put their available resources to use. A clear and identifiable statement of the broader institutional mission is essential in the academic budget cycle. Your responsibility is not so much to affect this process as it is to understand the timing of these decisions and the criteria or formula items on which they are based. It is not a good idea to request budget increases for new growth right after a "bloodletting"; on the other hand, you don't want to wait too long after a "transfusion" to request needed funding. Understanding the criteria used and being aware of these conditions in your current environment are important and will pay great dividends as you seek sufficient resources to support your department's priorities.

When an institution receives its budget allocations, either from the founders or the legislature, it then sets its priorities through the internal allocation of resources. Many institutions no longer allocate to all divisions equally but attempt to allocate to the various divisions, schools, and colleges on the basis of institutional goals and priorities (Grobmyer 2002). However, even when linking budgets to institutional goals, they will first set aside budget dollars for all continuing programs, mandated directives, and capital requirements. These are usually determined centrally from the institution's budgeting office and typically include current salaries and benefits, legislated increases, facility and utility expenditures, maintenance costs, goods and services, and the like. A second priority at the institutional level is the dedication of reserve funds for contingency purposes, in case of unexpected shortfalls and fluctuating formula data. It is the remaining resource base that will be available for differential distributions.

Your role at this level is more to understand the process than to agonize over the allocations. Remember, if the dean doesn't have it, the dean can't give it to you. If you want more insight into this process at your institution, make an appointment with your dean or your administrative financial officer. He or she not only understands the process but is probably eager to tell you about it.

General-Discipline Budgets (College/School)

It is at the college or division level that the allocation process begins to directly affect department operations. Deans or division heads must be conversant with institutional goals and be able to translate how the results from their units will contribute to these broader objectives. This is also your best opportunity to impact the budgeting process. Spend time understanding the dean's budget requests for the college. Do you understand or agree with the college priorities that are being articulated to the university? More importantly, what information can you give the dean to help identify and explain the desired outcomes (goals) valued by the college and the university?

Each dean faces the challenge of articulating a set of college or division outcomes that can assist the institution in "selling" the budget request to its public or private funding source. Budget priorities must be based on the principles cited in chapter 2: academic quality, financial need, goal centrality, and relative cost. Although these can be reported in relative terms (incremental or comparative), they need to be measured if they are to be managed. Can you provide any of these measures? As the dean requests budgets based on the measurable outcomes from your department, both the college and your department will stand a better chance of receiving the budgets to support those requests.

Refer back to Table 5.1 for specific examples of quantifying your enrollment and placement trends, service programs, research achievements, national and international recognition, community relationships, professional contacts, extramural funding, and so forth. A typical request for additional faculty lines, travel funds, or computer systems (even if everyone knows they are needed) makes it difficult for the university and the college to respond. Raising your programs to the level of national recognition, attaining financial support from an external constituent, forming active alliances with student recruiters, and providing service classes for the college or university are all measurable goals that will be valued by the institution and college and that can allow them to allocate additional resources to those ends.

You do not have the responsibility for college-level budget effectiveness, but you can improve your department's position if you can identify results from your department that will contribute to the college's goals and thus to those of central administration. Perhaps, at this level, department chairs need to understand the politics of managing as it relates to the criteria of budgeting. As you consider the increased needs of your budget over time and compare them to those of other institutions and departments, be sure you can articulate your department's advantages (goals, results, and outcomes) to your faculty and your dean. But also keep in mind that as your resources improve, you should be able to show the related improvements and growth in your measurable goals, results, and outcomes.

Operational-Level Budgets (Department)

As discussed earlier, each level of the budget process is concerned with both the request (resource acquisition) and the decision (resource allocation). Budget allocations at one level directly interface with budget requests at the next-lower level. Figure 5.1 shows this most important relationship among the five levels.

Just as the college budget is approached with the institution's values in mind, your department budget should be requested from the college's allocation perspective. Make your requests to the dean by showing measurable changes that you can achieve with those funds. Get all the information you can concerning the processes, resources, and goals at all levels. Prepare your department budget request with your dean's interests in mind. Find a way to present your faculty's plans and department's goals to show how they will provide support for the college's plans and priorities.

This is your best avenue for securing the necessary resources to support your department's priorities. Understanding the driving forces at each level in the budgeting process can greatly improve your ability to impact the process at your level and to communicate it more effectively to your individual faculty members (see Chemers 1993; Sparks 1999). Some examples of the measures driving the budget process at each planning level are listed in Table 5.2.

Table 5.2. Budget Level Outcomes

BUDGET LEVEL	EXAMPLES OF BUDGET MEASURES RECOMMENDED BY CURRENT RESEARCH
Level 1: Initial funding source	Private: endowment level, general financial health, student enrollments, funding successes Public: state economy, public interests, educational priorities, institutional competition, taxpayer intent
Level 2: Institution	Enrollment levels and student composition; faculty loads and tenure policies; aggregate salary levels; physical plant, library, computer, and other support facilities and services; external support successes
Level 3: General discipline (college level)	Faculty loads and salary levels, equipment and other support services, academic quality, enrollment trends, university service courses, extramural funding levels, national recognition, community relationships, development activities
Level 4: Department	Faculty productivity, staff effectiveness, equipment support, student enrollment, degree majors, research recognition, academic programs external support, internal service courses, development funding
Level 5: Faculty	Promotion opportunity, teaching and research support, travel budgets, lab facilities and equipment, teaching levels and loads, service requirements, graduate student assistance, grants and contracts, external contacts

Try to visualize your budget's relationship to the college in much the same way your faculty members relate their budget requests to the department. Document your budget requests with specific budget increases, and then provide your dean with the measurable changes that you can achieve with these resource allocations (see Rosser, Johnsrud, and Heck 2003). Help the dean allocate resources to your department by articulating the improvements to be achieved with these allocations. For example, a department request for additional faculty lines will be more helpful when presented in terms of measurable enrollment increases, program recognition, or extramural funding levels. Similarly, requests for travel funds or lab equipment are better received when promoted to attract new levels of research, external grants, or new gifts from private donors.

Providing such information to the dean is not an exercise in futility. It raises the dean's interest in your requests and it will improve the quality of the college budget requests to the university. Additionally, it will improve the relationship between the college and the department (not a bad side benefit) and give you more specific and useful budget information to share with your faculty.

Setting meaningful goals and identifying future expectations are difficult processes for your dean as well as for you. Both the dean and your faculty will greatly appreciate your ideas and assistance in this regard. This is the real value of the "strategic planning processes" that everyone keeps talking about (Hitt and Ireland 2002). It is important that you establish goals, identify future expectations, and determine priorities for your faculty and department before, not after, you make your budget requests.

Individual-Level Budgets (Faculty and Staff)

As shown earlier, department budget requests are directly related to college budget allocations, and faculty requests must be aligned with the department budget allocations. With input and communication from your faculty, the department budget is your responsibility. Much has been written concerning this budgetary responsibility, with many suggestions on how to communicate it effectively to staff and faculty. The perceptions of more than 280 faculty members from three separate institutions show that faculty generally do not perceive themselves as having adequate knowledge of the budget process, do not believe they are well informed on the current budget status, perceive funding as being inadequate at their institutions, perceive that they do not participate adequately in the budgeting process, perceive administrators to be uninterested in faculty participation in the budgeting process, and want a more active role in the budgeting process (Taylor and Kundy 1991, 8).

Thus, in general, faculty members feel that their current participation in the budgeting process is relatively passive, but they do desire a more active part in the process. Again, recognize this as your opportunity to impact the budget process.

Most department chairs seem to communicate budgetary matters to faculty after the fact, providing them with little information prior to or during the process. Others tend to overcompensate, providing detailed input and requiring faculty approval at each step in the process. Both of these extremes can contribute to negative faculty perceptions. Because faculty members are your primary sources of information concerning both goals and budgets, consider the following specific recommendations for getting your faculty more involved:

1. Have each faculty member present his or her needs (budget requests) in writing, with supporting justifications and, if possible, the measurable changes that will result from these budget requests. This preliminary step prevents faculty from submitting wish lists rather than realistic projections. It gives you valuable information concerning faculty members' plans and the impact they can contribute to future department outcomes. This is the strategic management process that is discussed in detail in chapter 6.

2. Schedule a time to individually discuss each faculty member's request. This step provides you with the opportunity to address possible alternative suggestions and to discuss goals informally, as well as to review faculty progress during the year (Kable 1992, 85). By focusing these discussions on measurable changes, you will increase the opportunities for effective budget allocations toward faculty successes. In making your faculty allocation decisions, you should (a) be informed of each faculty member's interests, accomplishments, and plans; and (b) share with them as much information as possible concerning the budget process at each organizational level.

Be sure your budget preparations and decisions are not primarily incremental or political but that they do take into account your college and department goals, the specific plans of each faculty member, and the accountability for achievements in relation to budgets. Chapter 6 further explores the strategic planning process and how it can be specifically used to motivate faculty and staff activities in relation to your limited resources. The department budgeting process that seems so irritating at times is one of your essential manager activities and can become your greatest tool to support your department leadership role (and perhaps even make it more enjoyable in the process).

Chapter 6

RESOURCE DECISIONS

— Planning Directs the Action —

> Never tell people how to do things.
> Tell them what to do and they will
> surprise you with their integrity.
> —George Patton

A colleague once wore a large, real carrot on a chain around her neck during a two-day management conference she was conducting. Of course, it generated a lot of raised eyebrows and many questions, but she wore it the full two days without any explanations. At the end of the session, she unchained that very large orange tuber and explained to the managers in attendance that she had been conducting an experiment. "I was told," she explained, "that carrots raise a person's energy level and improve the eyesight. But I now can tell you that it is just not true. I have been wearing this carrot all week, and it has not improved by even one iota my energy or my eyesight." With that, she tossed the carrot into the nearest trash can.

This is not a chapter about wearing your management role. It is a chapter about how to integrate, how to consume and digest the budgeting and planning process. Just knowing the techniques of management (wearing them around your neck) will not help you with anything; however, eating and digesting them (trying and using these ideas) will make a difference.

Allocating department resources sounds very administrative, but as you learned in chapter 5, your challenge as department leader is not simply administrative. You are faced with the daily interactions among your students, staff, faculty, dean, and other constituents, and this is the way it should be. This is, as they say, where the tires hit the road. All departments are busy, and all faculty members have trouble finding time to do everything they have to do—but your role is influencing how effective all of these activities are in moving your department toward its planned future.

GIVE DIRECTION

Daily discussions, interactions, and department decisions are most effective within the context of a planned future. Much of the literature on "organization or strategic planning" begins with discussions of mission and vision statements. Your department budgeting decisions are no different. A clear and well-communicated department mission statement should guide these decisions. This is how you begin to "taste the carrot." Just having an idea of your future is not enough. You need to articulate and share that vision with your faculty through a well-thought-out strategic plan and mission statement.

Your mission statement, an expression of planned future directions, need not be specific or action oriented; rather, it should constitute your guidelines for the department's future. In general, a mission statement should (a) articulate an image or visual conceptualization of your department, (b) provide an orientation to future department potential, (c) identify your department as a unique entity in a unique context, and (d) inspire your faculty toward excellence (Gmelch and Miskin 1993).

Visual Conceptualization

An effective department needs a picture of its end goals (its future potential) to guide plans and budgets. Your department mission statement should put into words your conceptualization of where the department is heading. Can your faculty "feel" or "see" the department's potential and how they fit into it? As a blueprint to the future, your mission statement needs to portray specific images of your department's long-term potential. Find out what is important to your university, to your college, to your faculty —then build your department mission to support, facilitate, and assist in moving in these directions. If the college has determined to accept reduced enrollments if necessary to increase student quality, your department goals may be misplaced if they are focused on increasing student numbers regardless of quality. Adversely, if your faculty has particular expertise in scientific exploration and building research alliances, setting department goals to increase the research support systems may be a critical link in the planning process.

Future Orientation

Department chairs must do more than just organize tasks, set goals, and meet short-term deadlines. They must provide their departments with an orientation to the future that correlates to the college goals and takes advantage of their faculty strengths. Young departments with relatively few senior faculty may need to be more research oriented until their faculty members mature to the broader services goals. However, if you have senior faculty with strong constituency connections, you may be best served with department goals to develop extramural funding sources and develop new partnership programs. Your staff and faculty will typically make their own plans based on a relatively short-term focus; your role is to provide a future-oriented framework to unite their daily activities to the more long-term department plans and budget decisions.

Unique Focus

As department chair, you must provide a meaningful context for your planning and budgeting decisions. What are the opportunities specific to your institution or department? What are the particular strengths and achievements of your individual and collective faculty? What unique services could you provide to students and constituents if you did have the resources to adequately support your faculty and department? Your role as chair requires the communication of a perspective unique to your department's present and future potential. Your mission statement should inspire your faculty's efforts toward a future unique to your department. This is not a "quick and easy" fix to the planning process, but it is essential to effective department leadership and will be discussed in further detail in chapter 7.

Inspired Excellence

Department mission statements are visions of the future intended to inspire creative and exciting short-term achievements. This requires chairs to be aware of the institution- and college-level mission statements. Do you know and understand the priorities of your dean? Can you create a contextual direction for your department that will assist the college move toward its future potential? But remember that mission statements are just that, shared directions for the future. It is your operational plans and annual budgets that will initiate and encourage effort and activity toward these goals. This beginning is imperative if you want your budget decisions to encourage faculty activities that are in the best interests of the department, the college, and the university.

ADD OUTCOMES

The concept of strategic management has been introduced, explained, and explored by researchers in many disciplines for many years. In essence, the concept of strategic planning follows the three main directives of identifying current status (where are we?), exploring internal strengths and external opportunities to determine future potential (where do we want to be?), and planning how to use resources to move us in those directions (how do we get there?). Richard Bowman (2002, 159) summarizes this strategic approach for department chairs as most useful "when they focus on the key aspects of organizational culture; mission, vision, engagement, and adaptability."

For your mission statement to be useful to you and to your faculty, it needs to be focused appropriately. Share your department mission statement with your staff and faculty, but more importantly, share your interpretation of the mission statement. For example, what do *you* mean by "distinctive" programs? Does "scholarship" include teaching and community programs, or is it limited to research and grants? How do you assess the success of your graduates? How do you assess the quality of your academic programs? How do you value the research and outreach results of your department and your faculty?

You can answer these and other questions by listing key outcomes (major areas in which results are vital to department success) specific to your department. For example, a general mission statement stressing nationally recognized faculty, high-quality graduates, and improved constituent relationships would be more easily communicated to faculty through a list that includes at least some of the following specifics:

1. Student learning measures that identify desired student achievements

2. Publication quality and numbers acceptable to and preferred by the college and university

3. Student placement measures desirable to the department and college

4. Academic program results that describe desired quality

5. Number and types of relationships to be gained and sustained with identified constituents

6. Levels of extramural grants and development funds currently targeted

By listing and identifying acceptable measures for the four to six key outcome areas critical to your department's mission, you will be providing initiatives that are vital to guide your faculty's efforts and your department's budget decisions.

The extremely fragmented and cumbersome nature of department chair responsibilities makes this step in the strategic planning process particularly useful. To illustrate this importance, take a quick look at the list provided in Table 6.1. This is an actual list of one chair's administrative duties during a typical week. Just a glance makes the week seem disjointed and almost overwhelming in nature.

Now, suppose this same chair was guided by a set of key outcomes emanating from the department mission. This same list of duties is shown in Table 6.2 with the visual prioritization of the major chair responsibilities (key outcome areas). The activities as listed in Table 6.2 are not fewer or less complex—but in the context of the departmental priorities, their value in encouraging faculty effort and allocating department resources becomes decidedly more clear.

Listing your own set of key outcome areas in the department mission statement with a shared set of measures to assess each of those priorities will give direction to faculty activities and improve your ability to communicate the value of your mission statement to both your faculty and your dean. What better guide for articulating department priorities, requesting college funding allocations, and setting department budget allocations?

CREATE GOALS

Some have labeled the managing of academic faculty as the "almost impossible mission" (Creighton 2001). The strategic process for department chairs is to link the university, college, department, and faculty together in a consensus-building and productive environment. In reference to this process, Creighton specifically asks the question, "[W]ith no carrot and no stick—how can you 'manage' faculty?" (41). To borrow from researchers in the business community, the strategic paradigm of directing, developing, and encouraging faculty success is perhaps one of our best answers to these questions (Amit, Lucier, et al. 2002).

As previously noted, a clear mission with desired key outcomes is the critical first step to inspire department unity and faculty excellence. The next step in the process, goal statements, are needed to focus on the shorter-term (usually annual) planned activities and to operationalize the department statements. By tying each department goal to one or more key outcomes in the mission statement, you begin to define the measurable achievements of highest value to your department and college. These measurable priorities are the step in the process that will inspire faculty productivity and should drive budget requests and budget allocations.

Even within the political context of budget decisions, department goals give direction toward department mission. However, when they can be related to key outcomes, they will give initiative to faculty effort and department potential. The basic premise of goal-setting theory seems obvious in its assertion that the conscious intentions of people influence their

Table 6.1. A Week of Administrative Activities Reported by One Department Chair

- Schedule classes.
- Meet with constituent groups.
- Assign new faculty to university committee.
- Set new department grading standard.
- Review complaint from unhappy student.
- Make field visit to company with new technology.
- Discuss qualification of recently hired student with recent employer.
- Order equipment to update lab facility.
- Schedule faculty meeting to encourage diversity.
- Send memo to encourage student participation in newly approved program.
- Send department goals out for faculty review.
- Coordinate summer school assignments.
- Generate list of development sources for the dean.
- Request additional resources to teach new class section.
- Compare national scores and results of department.
- Settle dispute between two faculty members.
- Invite special equipment vendor for campus visit.
- Approve student request for course waiver.
- Schedule regular faculty meeting.
- Send memo to encourage faculty to support student associations.
- Hire new department staff member.
- Invite new class offering from selected faculty.
- Telephone contact with advisory committee chairs.
- Review specific goals and plans with faculty member.
- Meet with faculty and student on cheating accusation.
- Assign faculty and TA loads for coming semester.
- Provide feedback to individual faculty member on problems with existing research plans.
- Request training seminar for instructional effectiveness.
- Ask for report on semester enrollments.
- Counsel deficient students.
- Counsel faculty member on effects of personal problem.

SOURCE: Adapted with permission from *Leadership Skills for Department Chairs,* by Walter H. Gmelch and Val D. Miskin (p. 49). Copyright 1993 by Anker Publishing Company, Inc.

NOTE: Notice the fragmented and disconnected nature of the activities as listed and the difficulty of remembering what each is trying to accomplish—let alone how to put them in any semblance of time or budget priority.

Table 6.2. Department Key Outcomes: Prioritizing a Chair's Activities

Improvements in the student learning outcomes area

- Plan seminar for instructional effectiveness.
- Review complaint from unhappy student.
- Discuss qualifications of recently hired student with current employer.
- Encourage students to participate in new program.
- Counsel deficient students.
- Meet with faculty and student on cheating accusation.
- Send memo to encourage faculty to support student association.
- Compare national scores with results of department.

Activities directed toward faculty achievement

- Schedule faculty meeting to encourage diversity.
- Settle dispute between two faculty members.
- Send department goals out for faculty review.
- Call and conduct faculty meetings.
- Provide feedback to individual faculty member on problems with existing research plans.
- Make faculty and TA teaching load assignments.
- Assign faculty to university committee.
- Counsel faculty member on effects of personal problem.

Developing and strengthening academic programs

- Set new department grading standards.
- Hire new department staff member.
- Invite new class offerings from selected faculty.
- Request additional resources to teach new class.
- Approve program requirements.
- Coordinate summer school assignments.
- Schedule classes.
- Ask for report on semester enrollments.
- Order equipment to update lab facility.

Building stronger relationships with constituencies

- Select advisory committees.
- Telephone contact with advisory committee chairs.
- Make field visit to company with new technology.
- Meet with constituent groups.
- Invite special equipment vendor for campus visit.
- Seek opportunities to recognize constituent groups.

SOURCE: Adapted with permission from *Leadership Skills for Department Chairs,* by Walter H. Gmelch and Val D. Miskin (p. 50). Copyright 1993 by Anker Publishing Company, Inc.

NOTE: Notice that each activity is placed in perspective as it contributes to a department outcome. This simple comparison makes day-to-day routines, problems, and decisions seem less fragmented and gives focus to time and budget priorities.

actions and behavior. But the real questions are: What actions? and Toward what ends? Conclusions drawn from the many goal-setting studies that exist today seem to agree that setting goals will improve performance to the degree that:

1. the goals are specific, measurable, and clearly stated;

2. the goals are set at high levels of achievement but still remain within the reasonable realm of attainment;

3. regular attention and feedback are provided; and

4. each goal is related to the attainment or improvement of planned organizational outcomes.

Department Goals Set Budget Priorities

Within the context of the key outcome areas identified in your mission statement, your department goals prescribe which accomplishments are important this year to you, your faculty, and your dean. They also establish measurable targets that can be achieved as you move toward the directions of the department and the college. Remember, too, it will be your budget decisions that will give life to these efforts and activities. You need to establish specific department goals based on the key outcome measures defined in your mission statement. Discuss these with your dean. Share these with your faculty. Review and assess these goals in relation to the four elements of effective goal setting described earlier.

Suggested goals for each key outcome area can be gleaned from the literature; we include some here as ideas on which to build your own set of department goals.

- *Student learning:* standardized score levels, student evaluations, admission ratios, placement data, program completion ratios, individual knowledge and skill development levels, alumni accomplishments, diversity of student body

- *Faculty achievement:* department publication record, faculty evaluation levels, department record of grants and grant proposals, student-faculty ratios, national recognition by discipline, relevance of academic programs, faculty-student relations, department teaching quality, community projects

- *Academic programs:* degrees and placement data, program evaluation systems, chair evaluations, levels of faculty involvement, department resource allocation and budget priorities, faculty goals, action plans

- *Stakeholder relationships:* coordination with other departments, activity with other colleges, relationships with government agencies, involvement with employer groups, membership in professional associations, joint programs with community groups, partnerships with private organizations

- *External grants and development funds:* network relationships, contract assistance, grant support systems, private contributions, successful grants

These are the measures that drive effective department budget decisions. These are the initiatives that can help you attract resources from the dean. These are recognitions that can assist your dean to request resources from the university. You must not only know what these goals are, but you should be sure your dean knows and agrees with their intent and direction. As with a carrot worn around the neck, if you don't find ways to get these data to your dean, you may never see the fruits of your labor.

Prepare and deliver progress reports as your projects move toward completion, send copies of media stories or other recognitions received by your faculty for their measurable achievements, prepare thank-you letters to department donors and contractors, publish student achievement results —these, and all others you can think of, should get to your dean's desk. These are critical communications to the strategic planning process and something that you should carefully and consciously make happen. Sharing successes with your dean is also an excellent way to share them with staff and faculty. This not only improves your chances of getting approval for your budget requests, but it also enhances the allocation side of your budgeting process. It actively involves others in your budget decisions and motivates faculty activity toward department priorities. Remember, your faculty are colleagues as well as experts in their respective disciplines; as such, they expect and need to be aware of the department goal-setting and budget allocation decisions.

CONNECT YOUR FACULTY

Reporting from an earlier study conducted with 18 different schools, Jane Huffman (2003) has gleaned two emerging purposes emanating from the strategic planning process. One area focuses on the development of trust and communication between administration and faculty; the second focuses on identifying specific areas for improving department results. Huffman strongly supports the thesis that it is the supportive conditions of trust and communications (the first purpose) that allow your faculty to successfully direct their efforts toward department goals (the second purpose).

As you review department goals, ask yourself, Who is it that will accomplish these goals? You will not be accomplishing them alone. The achievement of department goals requires the expertise, knowledge, and efforts of your faculty. Your challenge as chair is to involve your faculty actively in the implementation process, but it requires a strong dose of open communication and faculty trust. Achieving department goals is certainly desirable for all concerned, but you will need the willing participation (trust) of your faculty to find that success. Perhaps building this working relationship with your faculty can only come from their belief that you are concerned with their successes. The strategic planning process not only facilitates this trust but perhaps is essential to it. Remember, individual goals are your faculty's first priority—and rightfully so. These serve the interests of the faculty. These are their measures of career success. Your challenge is to find ways to make these individual interests, efforts, and achievements compatible with the achievement of your department goals (see Gmelch and Miskin 1993; Kotter 1990; Sparks 1999).

Universities, colleges, and academic departments widely report three basic categories of faculty assessment: teaching, research, and service. As we suggested in chapter 4, this list can be expanded to include citizenship. These are all important to the successful department, but some are more important than others to your individual faculty. All of these dimensions, you will note, are closely related to your departmental key outcome areas. These areas (teaching, research, service) can be considered as the key outcome areas for faculty effort and assessment. This encouragement, this understanding, this strategic link between department and faculty member is the key to connecting your faculty to this process.

Faculty Goals Drive Budget Decisions

Faculty budget requests are department allocations, department budget requests are college allocations, and college budget requests are university allocations. This understanding gives life to the strategic planning process for your institution and your department. Just as all colleges or all departments should probably not receive the same budget allocations each year, your budget allocation decisions should not be directed toward supporting equal activities for all faculty members.

Rather, your budget decisions should be used to encourage and support individual faculty goals that will have the greatest impact on department success. But how can you accomplish this if you have no observable idea of the college priorities or no measurable expectations for your department? As your faculty members become aware of your budget emphases —as they begin to recognize the consistent use of identified measures for college and department success—they will begin tailoring their plans and activities in those directions. And do not lose sight of how these measures, these recognizable successes, will improve your budget requests from the college and can even assist the college's budget requests to the university.

You must encourage faculty members to propose and plan their own goals—but in this process you must help them connect their goals to the priorities and plans of the department. Perhaps your greatest tool for building trust relationships with your faculty is to discuss with each individual faculty member some specific, observable measures in each faculty outcome area (teaching, research, service, and citizenship). A few suggestions to consider are listed here for each category.

- Teaching
  student evaluation scores
  student learning measures
  course load assignments
  actual class sizes
  class projects and independent study supervision
  new course development
  innovative teaching methods
  feedback from faculty colleagues
  statement of individual teaching goals

- Research
  ongoing research streams
  potential research topics
  number and types of publications
  number and types of papers presented
  number of grant proposals
  grant acceptance ratios
  research activity with students and colleagues at other
    universities
  statement of individual research goals

- Service and citizenship
  student advising/counseling quality and numbers
  industry relationships (numbers and quality)
  constituency outreach activities and projects
  professional leadership positions
  approved consulting activities
  college or university committee assignments
  department assignments and committees
  personal development activities
  feedback from faculty colleagues
  statement of outreach goals in relation to department goals

Department goals can serve you well in attracting resources. Faculty goals will improve your allocation decisions. But recognizing the value of budgets to direct faculty efforts (purpose number two) should not overshadow the vital need to accomplish purpose number one (building faculty trust). Requiring no measurable goals to accompany increased budgets is an invitation to lost productivity. But increasing measurable goal expectations with no budget growth is a long-term recipe for disaster. Carefully, openly, and candidly link budget changes to specific changes in faculty efforts, directions, and successes. And be sure those directions and successes are in line with the directions and measurable successes of your department.

As you allocate budget dollars for faculty staff support, additional lab equipment, or expanded travel budgets, reflect first on how your allocations will affect individual faculty productivity. You can improve the value of your budget dollars by knowing how they will encourage important faculty activities. Interestingly enough, these are the decisions that typically have the most impact on faculty effort and over which you have the most control. Knowing how you will measure faculty contributions allows you to exercise that control and build faculty trust. As you use individual faculty measures to set budget priorities, you will be in a position to develop faculty relationships by openly and consistently linking budget decisions to department priorities.

To this point, our discussion has focused on the development of individual faculty and department goals that contribute to the overall mission. Chairs are instrumental in setting department mission and goals. Allocated resources and faculty effort must then be directed to accomplish those goals. Clearly, goal achievement does not just happen, it requires definitive resource support and individual effort.

YOUR BUDGET DECISIONS

In an attempt to decrease the quantity and complexity of department administrative decisions, some researchers have suggested that the department budgeting process should be further decentralized, with the academic budgeting process taking place one level lower than previously described (Dooris 2002–2003; Mabry 1993). That is, rather than reviewing each request for faculty support, the chair gives an actual budget amount to each faculty member. Faculty members are then free to make their own choices about how to spend their budgets. Preliminary results in programs operating this way indicate not only a reduction in administrative time but measurable savings in the allocation of discretionary budgets. Initial results are beginning to show that decentralizing the budget process has the potential to:

1. reduce the number of budget-related decisions to be made by the chair,

2. reduce the number of faculty complaints concerning the equity of department allocations,

3. improve trust levels between chair and faculty, and

4. increase faculty output levels without respective resource increases.

Whatever method you use to make individual allocations, the most important decision is the level of allocation to each faculty member. You should not strive for equity in distribution. As noted by several authors, resources should be allocated more to encourage opportunities than to repair problems (Buckingham and Coffman 1999; Collins and Porras 1997; Drucker 1974). Whether you allocate your operational budget one item at a time or decentralize it among your faculty, determine the amount to be allocated on the basis of individual goals and plans (productivity) rather than equity or "squeakiest wheel." Directing your faculty members toward new or improved projects and publications is a great use for additional budget dollars. Initiating new teaching methodologies or developing improved instructional skills will have increasing impact on student learning and program recognition. Helping faculty members to improve their success at attracting extramural grants and contracts is an excellent way to allocate department resources.

This does not mean that only your successful faculty should receive budget support; rather, it suggests that you should use appropriate measures of success as the rationale for your allocations. When budget reductions occur and when budget increases are expected, remember that the "specifics" of your planning processes, when done effectively, become your most effective rationale for your budget requests and allocation decisions.

A Final Perspective

Effective resource budgeting at the department level often depends as much on your communication skills as your decision abilities. As you prepare your next budget request, ask yourself first if it reflects (and articulates) your department's priorities and measurable aspirations. Does it include an expression of the department's contribution to the college priorities? Are individual faculty allocations linked to scholarly achievement, teaching improvements, or student learning outcomes? Are additional lab facilities being used to attract extramural grants or improve student placement ratios? Do the increases in your operating budget show related increases in your department's academic reputation or measurable changes in student achievements?

Communicating the answers to these questions is more vital to the health of your department, perhaps, than the decisions being made. Measurable faculty outcomes and assessable department results will better represent your budget requests than either incremental or comparative expense data. Remember, your effectiveness in obtaining resources will rely as much on your rational articulation as on your political savvy. Don't approach your budgeting decisions as a "resource distribution," but rather as a "value-added" exercise. Keep your "manager" focus on allocating resources to direct faculty productivity toward recognizable department achievements.

Adding value is more productive than redistribution. As department chair, you will be faced continually with budget shortages and limitations —and occasionally, a budget increase. In either case, consider how these might be used as "opportunities" to initiate improvements and seek productive alternatives that might otherwise not be possible. Table 6.3 provides examples of typical problems in staffing, support, and equipment needs with ideas and examples of possible resource solutions using the value-added approach. The emphasis here is not on reducing costs, or even on continuing services, but on allocating resources where they can have the most impact on the future. Improve the credibility of your budget communications and increase the productivity of your faculty interactions learning to communicate budget decisions more openly.

Regardless of the process you use, you must try to maintain the integrity of your department's planning and budgeting processes. Review your department goals to determine your resource priorities. If an academic program or discipline is not identified as part of the department's planned future, do not continue the same level of resource allocation. If important stakeholders are seeking additional strength in identified fields, shift additional resources in those directions. Your role in the planning process is not simply to attract more resources but to show recognizable improvements in quality and effectiveness as you encourage faculty initiative. We all know, however, that this is easier said than done. It will not happen completely or quickly, but it is your challenge as department leader, which is the topic of chapter 7.

Table 6.3. The Value-Added Approach to Department Problems

There will always be a need to maintain or increase the quality of academic programs, increase faculty productivity, and improve student achievement. As department chair, you will have an impact on these outcomes as you set priorities and make budget decisions. Evaluate your priorities in terms of assessable department goals and allocate budget to your faculty in terms of measurable achievements in line with department successes. Several typical problems are listed here as examples, with suggested solutions made possible by looking for "impact and improvement" rather than "limits and reduction."

Problem 1: Unexpected faculty resignations that leave scheduled courses without instructors

Solution 1: Rather than first looking for new faculty lines, consider additional teaching assistant help, added pay for tenured faculty, semester course load tradeoffs, and so on. Then seek opportunities to cancel less-needed courses, shift the teaching and research loads of selected faculty, reallocate resources to programs with more demand, and so on. You may even see this as an opportunity to redirect faculty resources to other areas of priority in the department.

Problem 2: Last-minute request from your dean to teach off-campus or "electronic" classes

Solution 2: Again, your first solution may not be the need for more resources. Check for opportunities from any suggestions in solution 1. This may be a way to give special recognition for deserving faculty or to create new enthusiasm or new directions to a less-productive faulty member. You might also use this as the impetus to provide specialized training to initiate new research streams or seek external funding opportunities.

Problem 3: Need for faculty to teach in areas of expansion where existing expertise is not sufficient

Solution 3: Seek to add value rather than request resources. All of the previous suggestions should be considered, as well as the opportunity for more significant program shifts. Retrain and redirect faculty in declining disciplines. Be sure position replacements fit the new growth areas rather than continuing the problem in declining areas. Sometimes the trauma of budget reductions can provide opportunities for paradigm shifts in faculty activity.

Continued on the next page

Table 6.3. The Value-Added Approach to Department Problems, *continued.*

Problem 4: Need for faculty to contract additional research with relevant agencies

Solution 4: Carefully consider the many alternatives for redirecting faculty effort —special assignments, shifts in research/teaching loads, private funding sources, partnerships, joint programs, applied research opportunities, industry-sponsored research, faculty-professional exchange programs, supervised internships, invited campus visits, and so on—as you consider the solutions for this type of budgetary problems.

Problem 5: Need for additional support for community outreach projects

Solution 5: First, look to reduced costs through student employment, internships, part-time staffing, and so on. Then consider the opportunities for private funding, company-sponsored assistance, joint sponsorship, and the like.

Problem 6: Insufficient staff to maintain quality lab facilities

Solution 6: Consider the same solution alternatives listed for problem 5. Additionally, seek to take advantage of contributions from other divisions in your institution, student fees for improved student services, special fees for community service, matching expense programs, and so on.

Problem 7: Insufficient equipment and facilities for effective classroom instruction

Solution 7: Consider all of the previous solutions. Avoid turning to the first thought of reducing classroom effectiveness or increasing resources. The value-added approach to budget dilemmas suggests faculty training tradeoffs, program or discipline shifts, research and teaching innovations, private funding possibilities, joint programs, industry sponsorship, student fees for improved services, and anything else your faculty might dream up. This may be an excellent opportunity to improve the effectiveness and focus of your development support systems.

PART III

LEADER

Chapter 7

CHAIR AS LEADER

— Facing the Challenges —

> There are two ways of exerting one's
> strength: one is pushing down,
> the other is pulling up.
> —Booker T. Washington

So, how well have you been making your million-dollar decisions (your faculty)? How productive are the fruits of those decisions? Are you pleased with the direction and quality of your department? What is your department becoming? What is your department capable of becoming?

In several of our previous studies, we asked chairs what they would like their departments to look like in five years. The question frequently elicited blank stares and comments such as "I haven't really thought about it"; "I've been too busy with the daily routine of scheduling classes, allocating resources, and such"; "You mean I need to set the vision for the whole department?"; and "Oh, sure!" In other words, many chairs do not realize either their role in or the critical value of creating a plan (mission or vision) to lead their departments into the future. A decade ago, if you had talked about department visions, your colleagues would have thought you were hallucinating, but in today's rapidly changing environment, they are critical. Your role as manager was discussed as the "busy" part of your job— making the day-to-day decisions about resource allocations, faculty hiring and promotion decisions, curriculum issues, student problems, and so on. But these managerial activities underscore the importance of your leadership role in keeping things moving together and moving in the right directions.

What Is Leadership?

There are as many definitions of leadership as there are problems in the academic environment. But the differences between managing and leading seem to be at the core of these definitions. There seems to be agreement in current research conclusions that managing attends to effective budgets, tasks, and roles while leading focuses on the influences for direction and change (Aldag and Joseph 2000; Brown 2001; Conger and Benjamin 1999; Kotter 1990; Leaming 1998). But let us propose a formal definition that differentiates between the role of "manager" and your role as "leader." Adapting descriptions from the classic comparisons of Burns (1978) and Rost (1993), we offer the following definition:

> Academic leadership is an influence relationship between the academic leader and faculty members who intend real changes that reflect their mutual purposes.

This definition distinguishes the role of leader from manager in three important ways. First, it denotes that leaders direct effort toward some future end result. While it is important for these future results to be mutually valued, it is the chair as "leader" who provides the impetus to move in these directions (vision/mission statements). Managers are responsible for effective and efficient programs and systems, but leaders must turn faculty attentions toward future environments, capacities, and excitements of both individual and department potential.

Second, this definition requires that real changes be targeted for mutually valued future achievements. Leaders are aware of their environments. Leaders build relationships with constituents. Leaders are cognizant of competitor programs and successes. Leaders know the strengths and interests of their individual faculty members. Effective management may improve program development and delivery, but leadership motivates faculty and staff toward the greater challenges of preparing for the future.

Third, we recognize that academic leadership simply must be an "influence relationship." Faculty members typically do not sit quietly awaiting your next directive, nor do they usually respond quickly to suggestions for changing their teaching goals or research priorities. Not only is it less problematic to invite rather than direct your faculty to move in new directions, but it also likely results in better choices for new effort and direction. Current leadership literature largely agrees that organizations benefit from efforts to build "participatory frameworks and continual commitments to the shared values, responsibilities and rewards of group leadership" (Polglase 2003, 25). Bridges and Mitchell (2000) provide a solid explanation of their proposal for leading the change process. They propose the importance of this influence relationship from the leader's point of view by suggesting four important steps in the transition to new directions:

- *Purpose:* Why do this?
- *Picture:* What will the future results look like when we arrive?
- *Plan:* What steps need be taken to get us there?
- *Part:* What must the leader do to make this happen? (Bridges and Mitchell 2000, 35)

Conditions for Leadership

Faculty members and department chairs interact in the leadership relationship. The "influence relationship" mentioned in our definition is one between faculty and chair; it is a dual (two-way) and noncoercive influence. This reciprocal influence is based on interpersonal skills instead of organization authority and personal rather than positional power. This influence relationship is a natural and essential element of the academic community. But the faculty-chair relationship is not an equal partnership in the sense that both parties are not expected to provide the same expertise. The faculty-chair relationship is unequal in overall department responsibility and in the contributions to academic expertise, quality teaching, and recognized research. These latter elements are faculty contributions. Administration just cannot bring all of this to the table. But leaders must provide the role of encouraging, directing, and inspiring these contributions toward some desired future state. The responsibilities in this influence relationship may be unequal in the specific. They are all equally important and should not be different in their intent. Leadership requires "mutual intent" to create a changed future (department vision). Forged by the noncoercive nature of the relationship, mutual interests and purposes are ultimately necessary to guide faculty activities. During a recent department chair search, one dean was asked, "What will be your expectations of the new chair?" "The chair," responded the dean, "will be expected to move this department into its proper future." The challenge to the department chair is to "make a difference."

Our intent is to provide some operational ideas and suggestions to assist you in further developing your leadership interests, capacities, and successes. Let us begin these discussions with an exploration of the environments within which you operate and the leadership challenges faced by most department chairs.

The Leadership Challenge

In an earlier study, more than 800 chairs representing 100 different universities were asked to "explain the most significant problems facing them as department chairs" (Gmelch, Carroll, et al. 1990).

Their responses, some of which are listed in Table 7.1, reflect surprising commonality among all chairs. Their challenges, as reported, can be grouped into three major categories: resource challenges, strategic challenges, and faculty challenges.

Resource Challenges

Of all chairs responding, 26 percent noted specific resource allocation and budget problems. The statements reported in Table 7.1 summarize the commonality of issues in this area. It is noteworthy that these resource challenges directly influence both strategic processes and faculty effectiveness.

The criticism of burgeoning costs and deteriorating quality is increasingly heard from our publics (taxpayers, governments, sponsors, students, employers). Too often, academic administrators respond to these concerns by instituting more budget reductions, often at the expense of program quality. This may even take the form of proving how wrong these constituents were to complain in the first place. You should make an effort not to fall into the resource reduction trap with your budget plans. Think creatively before you propose cuts in service support of assistantship budgets, travel funds, time-slip assistance, photocopying, office supplies, or instructional materials. Instead, consider realigning existing faculty positions, phasing out declining academic programs, and supporting your community's shifting interests. These options are often less likely to reduce teaching quality and long-term commitments to department success. Across-the-board budget cuts have much more detrimental impact on the overall department with less opportunity to sustain or encourage pockets of excellence. Although these are difficult decisions, they are more conducive than most other alternatives to protecting quality and improving productivity.

As discussed in chapter 6, your challenge in managing department resources is to be aware of your faculty's ideas and concerns and then allocate and use your resources effectively to support individual faculty productivity toward the achievement of department goals.

Strategic Challenges

The highest reporting rate (28 percent) of responding chairs came with the strategic issues and problems. The essence of this category is illustrated by the comments shown in Table 7.1. One respondent summarized the strategic issues as "attempts to influence the department's academic program successes, faculty achievements, and stakeholder relationships toward an identifiable desired future potential." Does this sound familiar? This is the definition of department leadership. Do not underestimate the value of strategic planning. Hire good faculty, develop their interests and

Table 7.1. Most Significant Department Chair Challenges: Department Chair Comments Categorized by Major Issues (Top Responses)

RESOURCE ISSUES (26% RESPONSE RATE)	STRATEGIC ISSUES (28% RESPONSE RATE)	FACULTY ISSUES (21% RESPONSE RATE)
• Keeping track of current budget expenditures • Maintaining department quality with fewer resources • Funding faculty positions and salary support • Fairly allocating resources to faculty in difficult times • Funding new facilities and research space • Funding instructional support • Gaining fair allocation for the department from the dean • Obtaining extramural funding • Generating additional department resources • Securing outside support for the department • Finding new sources of funding • Stabilizing funding for the department	• Setting department priorities • Restructuring the department in these changing times • Developing stronger political support for the department • Reshaping our programs to meet new environmental demands • Increasing department visibility in the college • Attaining more responsibility and power from the dean • Building faculty support for department goals • Improving student quality and maintaining enrollments • Shifting our future focus from one academic area to another • Diversity hiring in the department • Handling politics within the department, the college, and the university	• Loss of talented faculty • Attracting quality faculty • Rewarding productive faculty • Faculty replacement • Encouraging and sustaining faculty diversity • Maintaining faculty vitality • Incentives for quality teaching • Building relationships with individual faculty members • Assigning equitable course loads • Healing irrational rifts among faculty • Conducting effective faculty evaluations • Continually increasing demands on faculty • Maintaining faculty morale

abilities, manage your resources, but remember—these activities must be directed in some way toward your department's planned future.

Department leadership focuses on the total organization. It looks beyond daily activities, programs and problems to the overall growth and development of the department. The critical role of department chairs is to develop and share long-term, future-oriented directions with staff and faculty. The strategic planning literature, in both business and education, finds strong agreement in describing the basic purposes and requirements of strategic leadership (Dooris 2002–2003; Gordon 2002; Grobmyer 2002; Lucas 1994; Purser and Cabana 1997; Thompson and Strickland 1998). Using the concepts of effective budgeting and managing, the strategic leadership challenge typically addresses these basic questions common to the academic environments:

- Where is the department now? (environment scanning and analysis)
- Where do you want the department to be in the future? (vision and mission)
- How do you plan to get there? (goals, budgets, action plans)

Environmental Analysis (Where Are We Now?)

To effectively plan for your department's future, it is essential to identify its "present." This requires two important, but separate, phases of analysis. First, know your department's strengths and individual faculty capabilities and interests. Strengths are defined as positive abilities and situations within your department, college, or university that will enable your department to take advantage of opportunities in the future. Which faculty members have strong research activities in process? Which programs are receiving special recognition? Which constituencies are providing department attention and support? How strong is your department team climate as discussed in chapter 2? The following specific elements should be reviewed systematically as you identify and articulate your department strengths:

- Open and meaningful communications with your dean
- Collaborative relationships with other department chairs
- Collaborative research and teaching activities among faculty members, both within and beyond your department
- Individual faculty achievements, successes, and planned activities
- Notable enrollments in department majors, minors, and other discipline specific areas

- Your anticipation and projection of department funding sources, both from the college and from external constituencies

Second, be aware of and have access to the external environments within which your department functions. Who are your relevant "stakeholders?" Enumerate your identifiable constituencies, competitors, collaborators, supporters, clients, and so on.

To successfully guide your department into the future, you must not only know but also be actively involved in these interactive relationships. Know your constituents, interact with your competitors, spend time with your stakeholders, develop relationships with your collaborators, and recognize your supporters. This is not "organizational politics"; this is developing relationships to plan for and build your department's future. Your measures of current success do not lie just in the quality of your students and your programs; success is also assessed by the strength of your important external relationships. This external analysis is for the purpose of identifying opportunities—opportunities for future successes and achievements. And look to your department strengths as the key to taking advantage of these identified opportunities. You need to recognize and utilize your most effective faculty member's research interests and teaching skills from your most successful programs. Consciously focus prominent faculty research goals on new department research initiatives. Provide incentives to encourage your best teachers toward department teaching aspirations. Build on existing student qualities to strengthen department relationships with eternal constituents. Utilize your best professional contacts to direct the department's commitment to community partnerships.

Your role is to specifically analyze your faculty achievements and department processes and then to plan how your department strengths might be organized to take best advantage of recognized opportunities identified from your ongoing environmental analyses.

Vision and Mission (Where Are We Planning to Be in the Future?)

Building a vision for your department is not accomplished only by assessing the external environments but by positioning your particular department configuration to best meet the opportunities in those environments. It is your role to tie your faculty research and teaching strengths to your department's long-term goals; to build on existing student quality to develop relationships with future employers; and to use current constituent support to create external partnerships, grants, and program funding.

Creating and articulating department vision requires frequent and consistent communication. A compelling commitment to a planned future will not be easily accomplished nor intermittently shared. Personal and informal references and explanations are essential to support a formal, written department vision/mission statement. As you prepare your department statement, do not be caught up in the finality of the process. Remember, it is your use of and reference to this statement, not the statement itself, that will provide direction and leadership to your staff and faculty.

Rather than worrying too much about the precise wording of this department "guide to your future," just try to make it simple and to the point. But be sure it includes the following four elements:

1. *Visual Conceptualization.* Effective department chairs build a picture of what the department potential will look like. They may not know exactly how they are going to get there, but they develop a clear idea of what the department is striving for. Can your faculty and staff "feel" or "see" this department potential and how they will fit into it? As a blueprint to the department, your shared vision/mission statement needs to portray specific images of your department's long-term potential.

2. *Future Orientation.* More than just organizing tasks, setting goals, or meeting short-term deadlines, department chairs have a preoccupation with the future. Staff and faculty will typically (and appropriately) operate in the shorter-term present. The written vision/mission statement, on the other hand, must conceptualize a future-oriented framework to unite the daily activities and decisions. While faculty teaching loads and specific course assignments must be determined each semester, a department focus to improve overall teaching effectiveness requires a two- or three-year planning transition. Individual faculty research time must be continuously encouraged, but a shift in department research paradigms will require three to five years of preparation and planning. Class size and number of sections offered are always immediate concerns, but anticipation of future student and employer interests reflects the need for longer planning horizons. How well does your vision/mission statement provide a context for the longer-term planning decisions for your department's future?

3. *Unique Focus.* Your department vision/mission statement should inspire thought, plans, and effort toward a future that is unique (and appropriate) to your department. It should encourage your staff to capitalize on specific department strengths to take particular advantage of opportunities identified in your relevant external environments. Interactions with your stakeholders and constituents not only increase your awareness but also can influence your relationships and build on the strengths of your faculty. The department vision/mission statement should be written to inspire your faculty toward a future both unique and specific to their individual strengths and interests. Does you vision statement avoid the use of general platitudes and generic aspirations? How well does it differentiate and distinguish your department's potential and its ability to contribute to the broader goals of your college and university?

4. *Inspiration.* Annual goals and individual goals accomplish short-term achievements (what is planned), while the vision/mission statement

provides the long-term context (what we can become). Department mission statements are visions of the future to inspire creative and exciting short-term achievements. They encourage options, alternatives, and expressions of optimism and hope in a future-oriented context. Carefully review your department vision/mission statement. Is it in writing? Has it been and does it continue to be shared with your faculty, staff, and stakeholders? Does it exude a sense of the ultimate, a hope for the future, a standard of excellence?

Department Goals (How Do We Plan to Get There?)

The vision/mission statement is intended to provide long-term direction and aspirations of the future, but for these to become useful to all stakeholders (faculty and staff included), they must be interpreted into the present. Leadership must focus on the future, but it must function in the present. The department goal-setting processes encourage effort and activity, but these goals must be aligned with the longer-term future potentials (vision/mission statements). From your visualization and articulation of the department's vision statement, specific, measurable, annual department goals must be identified to initiate activities toward mission achievement.

Developing your annual department goals will provide the important impetus to shift from the "organizational" to the "inspirational." Department goals can take any shape or wording usable to your situations. As you develop your department goals, be sure they serve their intended functions by ensuring that they:

1. relate directly to each element in your vision/mission statement,

2. identify your annual department priorities,

3. are stated in clear and measurable terms,

4. be understandable and available to all department personnel,

5. become guidelines for all budgeting, personnel, and faculty development activities.

Setting such priorities is essential for sharing the long-term guiding principles and concerns for everyone in the department. By performing an effective external analysis and knowing the particular strengths of your faculty and department, you can invite stakeholder involvement through a set of annual department goals. Be sure your department priorities are clearly identified and are openly shared with all interested parties. Measurable department goals are essential to move from the present toward the future.

Department vision and mission statements invite unity and inspire excellence. Department goals focus on the shorter-term (annual) planned activities to operationalize your plans. By linking your annual goals to one or more elements of the mission statement, you are defining the measurable achievements of highest value to your department and college. Simply stated, department goals express in writing which accomplishments are most important this year to you, to your faculty, and to your dean. To effect this, department goals must be clearly stated, challenging, and achievable during the upcoming planning year. Review your department goals to see if they are:

- directly related to department vision/mission,
- measurable and specific,
- challenging yet achievable, and
- communicated frequently and openly to faculty and staff.

Faculty Challenges

The final major challenge, reported by 21 percent of chairs, relates to obtaining, retaining, and motivating quality faculty. Most department chairs identified resource management as their biggest problem in meeting and achieving department goals. However, faculty-related issues quickly become your top priority as you realize that department goals are achieved only through faculty effort and productivity. Reported faculty issues can be divided into two general categories: recruiting and hiring quality faculty, and encouraging individual faculty productivity. These were the topics of chapters 2, 3, and 4.

These challenges are obviously linked to the level of available resources, but their connection to department goal achievement must also be recognized. Your faculty challenge is best described as that of improving the initiative and effectiveness of your individual faculty members and influencing their ideas and concerns so that they more directly contribute to department success.

Building a positive and productive department requires a conscientious application of time, effort, and desire. Be aware of your environment, expand your interests, seek and accept new ideas, and enjoy your position of leadership—these are the requirements for inspiring your faculty. Remember, your intent is not merely to set department goals and make routine operating decisions. Rather, your interest is to listen carefully to each individual faculty member in order to help him or her want to be productive. Get a good start, and then keep it going. Your first priority must be the growth and development of each individual faculty member. This is a mutual relationship in which noncoerciveness is required; your leadership challenge is to encourage faculty to have a "real intent" to impact the future.

FACULTY DIRECTION

In their discussion of strategic implementation problems, Beer and Eisenstat (2000) identify six "silent killers" of the success of strategic leadership:

1. Lack of attention (leadership intensity)

2. Lack of clarity (priorities)

3. Lack of unity (shared organizational purpose)

4. Lack of communication (shared values, key outcomes)

5. Poor coordination (consistent and open communication)

6. Lack of implementation skills (strategic goals and plans)

As you review your department goals, ask yourself, Who will achieve these goals? Remember, you cannot accomplish them alone. Achieving department goals requires faculty expertise and commitment. Leadership, then, is influencing individual goals to be congruent with department aspirations. Involving your faculty can be a delicate process. While the department vision/mission statement prescribes desirable achievements for all stakeholders, it is the individual goal that will always be your faculty's top priority. And that is the way it should be. As we have already noted, universities and academic departments widely report three basic categories of faculty outcomes: *teaching, research,* and *service.* These categories continue today as viable guides for encouraging specific goals with each faculty member.

These three dimensions, you will notice, are closely related to your department mission and goals, and it is this connection that is key to the process. Your role is not to set goals for faculty members but to encourage individual goals that support department priorities. As with any organizational effort, the key to department success lies in linking individual faculty goals to annual department goals. The chair (department leader) will typically initiate the department goals, but individual faculty members must be allowed to set faculty goals. Your leadership role is to share a vision of the future that will encourage, excite, and inspire them to set goals in support of the department.

Regular discussions with each faculty member are both desirable and essential to this process. Discuss department directions with individual faculty members but lead them to develop their own individual goals that specifically do the following:

- identify measurable challenges to be achieved by them during the coming year (teaching, research, service)
- relate to department mission and goals

- are in some type of written format

Individual faculty goals, as with department goals, must be measurable, clear, challenging, achievable, and communicated. Most important, this process provides a vehicle for you to discuss individual faculty effort and achievement. What better way to recognize faculty activities, encourage faculty efforts, or discuss faculty deficiencies? Individual faculty planning will vary by department as well as by individual faculty member, but it should begin with individually developed faculty goals for the coming year. Using these faculty-determined goals, you will be in a great position to positively and meaningfully discuss each individual's past successes and planned future activities as they relate to the department mission and goals.

FACULTY DEVELOPMENT

Department goals are established to support department mission, and the department mission is set to support college goals. But more important, faculty goals are intended to support department goals. As stated earlier, it is the faculty who will accomplish department goals, but only in proportion to their alignment and shared purpose with individual goals. Since department success depends directly on faculty achievement, the efforts, accomplishments, and development of individual faculty members become the chair's top priorities. Ann Lucas (1994, 45) found that in "colleges and universities with high-quality departments, professional development of faculty members is viewed as an important ongoing activity." She further suggests that department success is highly correlated with the two chair roles of "department leader" and "faculty developer." Purser and Cabana (1997) assert that productivity is highly correlated to involvement in the planning process. Strategic planning is not just a process conducted by the dean or chair but the clarifying of mutual purposes to guide goals and plans created by those responsible for implementation. Effective use of strategic planning gives autonomy, decision, and empowerment to faculty and staff. And empowering others motivates productivity (Block 1990; Hogan 1992; Kouzes and Posner 2003; Klein 1998). But empowerment requires capable and knowledgeable staff. What better place than the university to find knowledgeable and capable employees? It is this emphasis on faculty development that becomes the essence of department leadership and the secret to department success.

Goal-setting is the process of specifying direction and giving measurable benchmarks to communicate activity and progress toward those directions. Goals, however, do not offer explanations or prescribe procedures to accomplish these directives. Therefore, the faculty goal-setting process may be an important faculty motivator, but it does not provide the best system for faculty development. In a recent article, Kevin Polglase (2003) proposes that individual development requires feelings of ownership. The key to developing your faculty members is to engage them in the goal-setting process, but then to give them the autonomy (and responsibility) to determine *how* they will proceed to meet these challenges.

Setting goals provides benchmarks to progress and establishes unity between college, department, and individual successes. However, it is the determination of "how to get there" that gives ownership and motivates faculty activity. Many authors have labeled the process that initiates such effort and resource support as "action planning" (Drucker 1974; Gmelch and Miskin 1993; Gordon 2002; Polglase 2003; Purser and Cabana 1997; Randolph and Posner 1988; Thomas and Bainbridge 2002; Thompson and Strickland 1998).

In simple terms, an action plan states the specific and sequential activities required to accomplish a given goal or objective. It further identifies the individual responsible for each activity and the specific time frame within which each step will be completed. Action planning forms such as the one depicted in Figure 7.1 are commonly available in most formalized management programs and are self-explanatory in nature.

ACTION PLANNING FILLS THE GAP

It has been said that action planning is more closely related to planning and budgeting than to goal setting. Action plans can clarify priorities and implement accountabilities. Action planning provides three visible benefits to you, your faculty, and your department by:

- Encouraging initiative and impetus toward individual goal achievement
- Improving communications at all levels
- Giving meaning to priorities for budget allocation decisions and resource requests

Initiative and Impetus

Action planning helps faculty members find starting points (impetus) for their individual goals, especially if they are not quite sure how to begin. It determines the specific steps, proper sequence, and appropriate time frame of activities to accomplish a given goal. Preparing an action plan not only identifies and approves the actual first step but also actively includes others in the process if that is desirable. For example, new faculty members who need to upgrade the quality of their research publications may not know the best way to approach this task. By encouraging them to develop action plans, you will not only see the expected results from your budget al-

Figure 7.1. Sample Action Planning Form

ACTION PLANNING

Goal or objective to be achieved:

_____
_____
_____
_____

Action Plan

Steps Required or Planned to Accomplish this Goal	Expected Completion Dates	Who Will Be Accountable for Each Step
1.		
2.		
3.		
4.		
5.		
6.		
7.		
8.		
9.		
10.		

locations, but you will encourage results through their identification of initial development steps, journal options, co-authorship potentials, colleague review panels, and even specific writing schedules.

Improved Communications

Action planning allows individuals to solicit ideas and suggestions on how to approach difficult goals or goals that they have not yet experienced. It also encourages them to communicate progress toward goals that may otherwise be difficult to evaluate. Faculty members who have been challenged to improve their teaching, for instance, might not be open to critique or suggestion from others—but they may be willing to seek assistance in the process of developing action plans "at their own initiative." If progress or improvement is slower than anticipated, the activities identified in the action plan can be shown as measurable improvements or reviewed for new ideas and suggestions. Action plans can accomplish great results when prepared by your faculty and can be a great tool for improving goal-oriented communications with your faculty.

Resource Priorities

Action planning provides an excellent vehicle for explaining your resource requests or building rationale for resource allocation decisions. Chairs faced with the difficult decision to reduce department budgets are likely to make more informed decisions if important faculty requests are accompanied by action plans that detail the steps, time frames, and accountabilities, as well as results to be achieved. Action planning is intended to encourage individual effort, improve communication among individuals, and provide resources to support individual goal achievement. These are the data that should guide your tough resource allocation decisions.

For Faculty Eyes Only

Faculty goals are best developed by individual faculty, but they need chair approval to receive departmental support. Resource allocations put teeth into the process. More important, this approval is part of the mentoring process and can become your check to ensure department and individual goal alignment.

But action plans are neither necessary nor desirable for every faculty member—or for every resource request. Action planning is best used when it is suggested or encouraged rather than required. Faculty action plans are "for the use and benefit of the faculty member." Action plans tend to lose their value when they are perceived as merely more close supervision or another chair control method. We suggest that you review faculty action plans only when invited. Decisions about how to accomplish individual goals should remain a faculty prerogative; remember, your faculty members provide the expertise and the initiative. Faculty members who elect to use action plans can use them to help themselves get things moving or to show progress toward a yet unachieved goal. It is always tempting for the chair to require action plans from faculty members who are particularly in need of some kind of help, but you should keep in mind that *this tool works best when the individual chooses to use it.*

Encourage action planning for faculty members who desire or are in special need of mentoring assistance for starting new activities encountered at their current career stage. You can suggest the action planning process to faculty members when they ask for (or need) help in starting new initiatives. You can recommend the reporting of action plan steps from faculty who desire to report progress on ongoing projects. You can introduce the value of action plans to faculty who need assistance in gaining additional time or funding for important projects. Action planning can always be recommended, and you can assist, support, and offer suggestion to the faculty action planning process. But to be effective, action plans must be faculty driven. As department chair, you should recommend action planning for faculty members as you judge necessary or helpful. Action plans can encourage and assist individual performance, and you will find them to be excellent tools for communicating budget requests to your dean and budget decisions to your faculty. If you use action plans wisely, your department relationships will become more productive and the long-term direction of your department will be easier to influence.

BUDGETING AND PLANNING AS INTEGRATED PROCESSES

Department leadership requires active participation in preparing for your department's future. Using the following outline can help you start now to integrate and operationalize the planning and budgeting process in your department.

- Develop a department vision (department mission statement) that includes a visual conceptualization of your department's potential, an orientation to the future rather than attention to the problems of today, and a focus on your department's and faculty's unique characteristics, with targets for change that inspire faculty effort and activity.

- Set department goals and identify measures that will give visibility to student achievement, faculty accomplishment, academic program quality, stakeholder relationships, and development successes.

- Encourage individual faculty goals that provide impetus for faculty activities in direct relation to department mission and goals.

- Connect faculty goals by encouraging faculty members to develop specific plans for achievement in their individual teaching, research, service, and relationship-building goals important to the department.

Your leadership role is to direct and develop faculty through their active (and appropriate) involvement in budgeting and planning. From the initial funding source of the institution through the college and department plans and allocations to the development of individual faculty, your ability to lead depends on your success in influencing and supporting those accomplishments that have the greatest impacts on department future.

Recognize the budgeting process for what it really is: an important tool for developing faculty and achieving goals. Department goals provide direction, individual goals create initiative, and action plans develop faculty.

In a recent chair leadership seminar, it was suggested that too much emphasis is being given to managing "results" and "outcomes." Criticism was expressed that helping faculty to achieve better results may set useful goals, but it does not help faculty get any better at meeting them. According to some of today's management consultants, more direction is needed to help faculty develop their teaching and research skills. We agree. This is your leadership role. Your greatest opportunity for impact lies in the support, encouragement, coaching, mentoring, and development you offer individual faculty. Recognize your stars, reward your horses, develop your newly minted faculty, and reposition your drones. While they may not all want your attention and may not need your assistance to the same degree, they will all benefit to the extent you can plan and guide resources to support individual faculty productivity.

LEADER OF INDIVIDUALS

As you make decisions that shape and influence your department's future, encourage faculty initiative and provide support for faculty members' successes. Individual faculty achievement is the heart of department activities, but faculty must operate within the scope of the department's planned goals. Effective department chairs have a clear role; they are the ones who light the way and, in the process, let everyone else know the value of their individual contributions (Miskin and Gmelch 1985). You must be willing to establish budget priorities rather than settle for equality in all allocations. Rather than focusing on reducing faculty differences, you should celebrate and develop their individuality. Plan for and influence resources and goals that contribute to the growth and development of your faculty and your department. Don't worry about deciding whether your first priority should be resources, faculty, or department goals. Rather, be aware how these elements can work together to encourage faculty productivity and more positive department results. Integrate faculty ideas to develop individual goals, support them sufficiently through active coaching, mentoring, and budgeting, but give them the autonomy (action planning) for achieving their own results.

Leadership listens to and encourages, it guides and inspires, it directs and empowers. Leadership brings health and vitality to the organization. It relies on active (but noncoercive) influence between faculty and chair. Remember, you are the leader of individuals. Don't just reflect on the ideas about developing faculty—try them out. Bring them to life with the resource planning and budgeting concepts discussed in chapters 5 and 6. It is our belief that leadership is not a trait or characteristic but that it is an influential relationship between you and your faculty members who intend real changes that reflect your mutual purposes.

PART IV

SCHOLAR

Chapter 8

CHAIR AS SCHOLAR

— The Paradox of the Swivel Chair —

> What I dream of is an art of balance, of purity and
> serenity devoid of troubling or depressing subject
> matter, . . . a soothing, calming influence on the
> mind, something like a good armchair which
> provides relaxation from physical fatigue.
> —Henri Matisse

Chairs often feel trapped between the conflicting roles of scholar and the
previously discussed administrative roles of faculty developer, manager,
and leader. Trying to look in two directions, they mediate the administrative concerns but at the same time try to champion their scholarly pursuits.
As a result, they find themselves swiveling between their scholarship interests and their administrative responsibilities. In essence, they are caught in
the role of Janus, a Roman god whose two faces looked in different directions at the same time. Although chairs need not worry about being deified,
they do find themselves in a paradoxical position, in a middle management
role that has no parallel in business or industry, or in education, for that
matter. Like no other managers, they must attend to their fiduciary responsibilities at the same time they must work to protect their personal scholarly interests. To balance these two roles, chairs must learn to swivel
without appearing dizzy or schizophrenic.

Although the conflicting roles of department chairs have received
some anecdotal attention recently in speeches, professional papers, popu-
lar journal articles, and how-to books, few data-based studies have investi-
gated the chair's swivel dilemma. Researchers know more about "the
motives, habits, and most intimate arcana of the primitive peoples of New

125

Guinea or elsewhere than [they] do of the denizens of the executive suites" (Mintzberg 1973, 7). Rarely do we study impediments to attracting academic leaders to the smallest, yet most significant, unit in the academy, the academic department. Nearly 80 percent of all administrative decisions take place at the department level (Carroll and Wolverton 2004). Academicians study many other professions but seldom investigate their own (Gardner 1990). As John Gardner, former secretary of the U.S. Department of Health, Education, and Welfare, aptly stated, "Education is to professors as water is to goldfish: They swim in it but never think to study it."

As the Chair Turns

Two ethnographic researchers followed department chairs around for weeks, much as an anthropologist would investigate a tribe in New Guinea (Gmelch and Seedorf 1989). Their observations provide interesting insights into what chairs do—not in the sense of the roles they perform but in terms of activities that make up the chair's day. Of particular significance to the chair's paradoxical problem of performing scholarly activities while attending to managerial tasks is the fact that a chair's work is characterized by (a) an unrelenting pace; (b) brevity, variety, and fragmentation; and (c) a preference for live action.

The Unrelenting Pace

The chairs they studied took very few breaks during their normal office hours, as they plowed through the mail, telephone calls, meetings, and other hurried activities that consume every spare moment of their time from their early arrival until office closing hours. It is at this time that they finally find refuge from the deluge of their managerial and leadership tasks. They can shut their doors, straighten up their offices, and cherish the solitude for reflective thought.

Presumably, one of the major reasons for the unrelenting pace of the chair's life is the open-ended nature of department administrative responsibilities. A perpetual preoccupation with work results from the chair's never having the pleasure of knowing, even temporarily, that his or her work is done.

Brevity, Variety, and Fragmentation

Chairs log dozens of written and verbal contacts daily, each dealing with a distinct and separate issue. Telephone calls average 4 minutes each; scheduled meetings, 50 minutes; unscheduled meetings, 7 minutes; informal tours down the faculty office corridors, 9 minutes; and sessions of uninterrupted desk work, 9 minutes. No wonder scholarship never emerges during the workday; 9 minutes is hardly enough time to germinate an idea, let alone to conceptualize a scholarly thought. This type of fragmentation and brevity challenges chairs' ability to perform even their leader and faculty developer roles.

For most chairs, morning activities cannot be distinguished from afternoon work. Even the same activities that are done daily do not take place at specific times during the day or on consistent days of the week, except when chairs teach classes or at the beginning or end of academic terms. Overall, how does a chair spend his or her typical day? The study indicated that seven-tenths of the chair's day is spent in meetings (47 percent in scheduled meetings and 22 percent in unscheduled meetings), 6 percent talking on the telephone, 9 percent taking office tours, and 15 percent sitting at a desk, solving problems, entering data into a computer, reviewing mail and memos, or carrying out other management duties (see Figure 8.1). Note that this study was conducted in 1989, prior to the onslaught of e-mail and the additional fragmentation of the chair's day with this new communication device. Chairs estimate that they spend one to two hours on e-mail a day and receive approximately 40 to 60 incoming messages.

Thus, the brief encounter with each activity, the variety of activities, and the lack of any activity pattern (with the exception of teaching and semester cycles) require department chairs to shift gears quickly and frequently. In effect, chairs lose the pleasures of blocking time to prepare for classes, exploring new ideas in their fields, and pumping out articles. Instead, they rush from one committee or task to another, day by day and week by week, and rarely receive satisfaction from completing a rewarding scholarly task.

Preference for Live Action

The chair's work environment is one of stimulus-response reactions, and it infrequently allows time for planning, reflective thought, or meaningful exchanges with colleagues. Compared with when they were faculty members, chairs spend less professional time teaching, writing, conducting research, and keeping current with their disciplines and less personal time with their families and friends—and they are not happy about it (Gmelch and Seedorf 1989).

The nature of managerial work for chairs resembles that of executives (Mintzberg 1973) and school superintendents and deans (Jackson 2002) —characterized by unrelenting pace, brevity, variety, fragmentation, and constant live action. However, these other professional managers are not also forced to scrape for blocks of time to maintain their status as scholars. From other research at the Center for the Study of Academic Leadership, we have discovered how passionately chairs feel about keeping their hands in scholarship. For many chairs, this is their most comfortable role, but one

Figure 8.1. A Day in the Life of a Department Chair: Brevity, Variety, Fragmentation, and Live Action (distribution of hours and average minutes per activity)

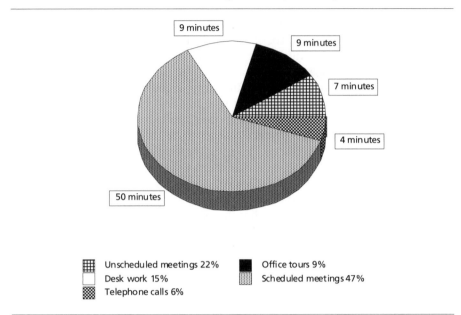

	Unscheduled meetings 22%		Office tours 9%
	Desk work 15%		Scheduled meetings 47%
	Telephone calls 6%		

that, as they serve as department chairs, causes them the greatest dissatisfaction, stress, and ambiguity.

THE SEARCH FOR BALANCE

Scholarship plays an important part in the lives of department chairs in all institutions. The definition of the chair's scholar role may vary from institution to institution, but most chairs find it to be their most enjoyable role. However, as we have noted, the demands of the job make finding time for scholarship virtually impossible. In one study, 86 percent of department chairs surveyed reported that their other chair responsibilities had caused them to reduce their scholarly activities significantly, and for some, scholarship essentially ceased (Moses and Roe 1990). We asked hundreds of department chairs in our study the degree to which they agreed or disagreed with the following statements:

- Chairs should have their load lightened to make more time available for research, writing, or other work in the field.
- If I saw no opportunity to do my own personal research, I would find my job less satisfying.

128

What would your responses be? Some 85 percent of the chairs we surveyed agreed with both of these statements (Gmelch, Carroll, et al. 1990). This may provide a clue as to why chairs swivel.

WHY CHAIRS SWIVEL

Chairs are socialized as scholars first. Their socialization begins in graduate school and runs through their time in the faculty ranks for more than 18 years before they move into the position of chair (Carroll 1991; Carroll and Wolverton 2004). How long does it take for a faculty member to metamorphose into a chair? Some 40 percent of prospective chairs report that they expect to feel comfortable in their new role immediately. Another 45 percent predict they will be comfortable in six months to a year. Only the remaining 15 percent of chairs expect that it will be more than a year before they become adjusted. This is amazing, given that these are the same people who spent almost two decades adjusting to and feeling comfortable in their faculty roles. In reality, the drastic differences between the roles of scholar and administrator make the transition to department chair a difficult one. As this transformation takes place, the new chair needs to change several "faculty" work habits, including the following.

Focused Effort. Faculty are able to block time to prepare for classes, to teach classes for hours without interruptions, and to concentrate on writing journal articles and books. The job of the department chair, in contrast, is characterized by brevity, variety, and fragmentation.

Discipline Orientation. After years of preparation, faculty enter the classroom to profess and disseminate information in a manner that meets the learning objectives of their students. As faculty turn to administration, they learn that success in the roles of manager and leader rests in the ability to profess less and to practice the arts of persuasion, rhetoric, and compromise.

Faculty Autonomy. Faculty enjoy control over their time and the feeling of autonomy of activity and movement in their academies. Faculty feel they pay the price for autonomy in the form of lower income, whereas department chairs receive a salary adjustment for their administrative work. However, chairs lose some of their faculty autonomy as they become accountable to mandates from central administration, edicts from the dean, and demands from faculty who want to find chairs in their offices ready to serve their needs.

Creation of Knowledge. Faculty are often used to having long periods in which to prepare manuscripts before their labors see print, but chairs must cope with fragmented times for writing, whipping out memorandums to persuade colleagues and create action.

Solitude. Faculty typically work alone when preparing for classes, teaching classes, reviewing literature in their disciplines, and developing projects. Department chairs must answer to numerous publics: students, faculty, parents, public agencies, and other administrators. To fulfill their manager and leader roles, they must work with and through their publics.

Customer Service. Faculty members are at the receiving end of services. Chairs, in contrast, become custodians and dispensers of services, materials, and resources. As one faculty colleague commented, "Chairs are there to provide faculty with the tools so they can do their jobs." A cartoonist whose work appears in the *Chronicle of Higher Education,* Vivian Scott Hixson, recently quipped: "George would make a great chairperson. He's the only one in the department who could plaster and paint the walls and repair the office furniture!"

In summary, when faculty transform into chairs, their roles and duties typically shift in several ways: from a focus on scholarship activities to a focus on fragmented meetings and interruptions; from a feeling of autonomy to pursue their own interests to a feeling that both faculty and administration control their time, activities, and actions; from professing in the classroom to persuading in meetings and political arenas; from a solitary work style to social collective action; from receiving department resources to allocating resources; and from writing manuscripts (such as this book) to writing memorandums.

SWIVEL BURNOUT

The work of administration and the work of scholarship do not make good bedfellows because the conditions needed to create scholarship are different from those needed for administration. Chairs are subjected to the stresses and pressures of performing not only their administrative role but their scholarly one as well. This dual pressure of the chair position is confirmed by a comparison of the most serious stressors of chairs with those of faculty. In our study of 800 chairs and 1,200 faculty, almost 60 percent of the chairs reported suffering from "heavy workloads" (Gmelch and Burns 1993), compared with 40 percent of faculty (Gmelch, Lovrich, and Wilke 1984). Not only do chairs retain the greatest faculty stressors, those of their scholarship role, while holding the chair position, they also add managerial pressures. Many chairs eventually suffer burnout from the strain of trying to be effective administrators as well as productive scholars.

THE LIFE OF SWIVEL CHAIRS

The career paths of department chairs are highly predictable. On the average, chairs' timetables follow the pattern of receiving a bachelor's degree at the age of 22, then master's degree (age 25), and doctorate (age 30).

They take the position of assistant professor at age 30, then associate professor (age 35), and on to tenure (age 35) and full professor at the age of 40. Then, after serving in the rank of full professor for six years, they accept the chair position at age 46. This pattern is less likely to hold true for women, who are older than men at most of their career events, but younger than men when called to leadership, and many times, before being promoted to full professor (Carroll 1991).

Not all chairs make a complete transition to department leadership and find balance with their scholarship. In fact, few chairs are fully socialized into administration (Seedorf 1990). After an average of six years of service, approximately one out of five chairs continues in academic administration and completes the full transition from faculty to administration, leaving scholarly agendas behind. However, most chairs (65 percent) do not complete the transition; instead, they return to full faculty status and remain there until retirement (Carroll 1991).

Essentially, department chairs follow two types of career paths: Administrator chairs move into the position of department chair as an entry into the administrative hierarchy of academic institutions; faculty chairs provide temporary service to the department and return to faculty status after their tenure as chairs. Although these paths reflect typical patterns for four-year institutions of higher education, they differ according to type of institution, discipline, and gender.

For many, there are no easy answers concerning where to turn next. But, as the Cheshire cat told Alice, if you don't know where you are going, any road will get you there. Here are some practical signposts you should read when traveling down the road to academic leadership.

- *Wait until you have been promoted to full professor before you seek the chair position.* Most deans will tell you how difficult it is to promote faculty members while they are serving as chairs. As one dean of business and economics explained to us: "I accepted the faculty's recommendation to appoint an associate professor to the chair position. Then, he came up for promotion three years later after a dearth of scholarship because of his administrative load. I'd like to reward him for his loyalty and departmental leadership, but now I face a dilemma since his 'papers are not in order.' "

- *Never accept the chair position before you are tenured.* For many of the reasons just stated, even more critical than rank is the importance of being tenured before serving as department chair. Normally, chairs can influence faculty through several sources of power: through authority vested in the position, through their ability to provide rewards or punishments, through their knowledge and skills, and through personal persuasion. However, tenured faculty members will be able to override an untenured chair's influence with their exceptional power as tenured members of the academy.

- *Accept the chair position early enough to keep your options open.* If you accept the position late in your career and then decide you really enjoy the challenges of leadership, you may limit the choices in your future career path.
- *Accept the chair position late enough so you have had time to establish your credentials and credibility.* Faculty look to department chairs as role models in many facets of faculty life, so you need to be experienced and trusted by your colleagues in order to support them and advocate their advancement.

REDESIGNING THE SWIVEL CHAIR

Some of the design problems of the swivel position are structural and inherent in the way colleges and universities are organized; others are personal and are rooted in how we manage ourselves. Higher education will continue to have a "leadership crisis" as long as chairing a department remains an unmanageable and unproductive option for faculty members. Solutions to the problems of attracting and retaining effective department leaders may lie in how the chair's position is structured and how the chair's time is used (Hecht, Higgerson, et al. 1999). We must create qualities that make the chair position more attractive, tenable, and meaningful for promising professors.

From your perspective, that of the department chair, all four roles must be viewed as parts of a single position rather than as separate entities. They must be in balance and harmony. The four roles can be compared to the four legs of a sturdy chair. One of the legs represents your ability to control your time; the second leg, your ability to manage the activity trap; the third, your ability to develop a hardy personal profile; and the fourth, your ability to create a golden parachute for yourself so that you can land safely after the journey into academic administration. Together, these four legs hold up a chair that is sturdy and stable. If any one of the four is weak, broken, or out of position, it affects the utility and effectiveness of the other three and the balance of the entire chair.

Control Your Time

Take time to learn—to save time. Develop an efficient working environment so that routine paperwork can be handled by office assistants, telephone calls can be screened, and time can be blocked into uninterruptible periods for reflective work. Find the system that works best for you. Listed below are a few time savers some chairs have found helpful.

- *Develop a dictation habit.* One of our colleagues swears by the Dictaphone: "I dictate all my correspondence and memos. It saves time but also saves physical wear and tear. . . . You can do it with your feet up on the desk, you can do it walking around the office, or you can go outside and walk around the campus grounds. You can't do that when you're typing." He drops off his dictated tapes for his support staff to transcribe and follow up.

- *Get hooked on the Internet.* Although some resist it, electronic mail is an invaluable communication tool. It allows you to keep in touch with widespread colleagues economically and efficiently. You just need to know how to separate the treasure messages from the trash.

- *Separate work and nonwork activities.* One of the most difficult challenges chairs face is that of leaving administrative work at the office at the end of the day. As we have noted, when professors move into the position of department chair, they develop dissatisfaction from their loss of time for scholarship and personal time for family and friends. Chairs need to take special care to separate their administrative work from their scholarly work, and their professional from their personal lives.

Manage the Activity Traps

Many chairs seem to fall into a trap of endless activity. We have noted that chairs' work is characterized by brevity, variety, and fragmentation; this often results in what seems to be a bottomless activity trap. When we first asked chairs where their problems lie, they typically cited externally imposed time wasters, such as endless meetings, unrealistic demands from the dean, interruptions, and drop-in visitors. However, upon further discussion, they realized that their true time wasters are self-imposed: unrealistic time estimates, failure to delegate, lack of planning, unclear vision, self-interruptions, and lack of concentration. The challenge, then, is to focus on what is important (Gmelch 1996b).

- *Concentrate on HIPOs.* How can chairs manage the activity trap? The typical time-saving scenario begins with a list of tasks in most efficient order. The trouble with this "to-do" list mentality is that it does not eliminate any tasks; it just reorders them. Instead, we recommend that you begin by putting away your list. Now, with a clear mind, write down three to five make-or-break, high-payoff tasks (HIPOs). If you have a mission statement with key outcome areas (see chapter 6), HIPOs should be easy to identify. Think about how each activity relates to these key outcomes. Every activity facing you will be important, but your choices about where you spend your time and effort will be more effective when you give priority to such activities as setting up a faculty search process, building your department budget, taking time to reflect on your department's future, and working with faculty.

- *Delegate/eliminate LOPOs.* Most chairs will not have difficulty identifying their HIPOs, but really breaking out of the activity trap also depends on your ability to identify and eliminate low-payoff activities (LOPOs). HIPOs should take precedence over the LOPOs of "administrivia" such as unimportant meetings, the writing of unnecessary reports, and responses to meaningless correspondence. Let the importance of tasks dictate your activities.

Maintain a Hardy Profile

Under the pressure to perform these multiple roles, why do some chairs collapse and others cope? A few clues from psychological research have emerged that help account for the resilience of some managers. Resilient managers, compared with nonresilient managers, tend to believe they are more in control of the events in their lives, have a greater sense of commitment to life beyond their profession, and view changes as challenges (Pines 1980). To these three qualities we add a fourth, humor. Here are some suggestions for how you can build hardiness into your life as a chair.

- *Develop a commitment to your profession and community.* Hardy chairs deal with the swivel effect by finding balance between their disciplines and their personal lives. They actively seek opportunities and options in their academic careers while maintaining their dedication to their families and communities.

- *See change as challenge.* Hardy chairs see problems as opportunities or challenges. However, they do not meet these challenges without restraint. They take risks, though not excessively, and feel that if they are not making mistakes every now and then, they are not really trying new opportunities. Change can be the spice of life, if it is handled right.

- *Take control of your destiny.* Hardy chairs believe they can have an impact on their departments and colleges. Rather than thinking that the bureaucracy or legislature controls their destiny, they identify and try to affect the events under their control.

- *Find the humor in the situation.* Hardy chairs take their jobs seriously but take themselves lightly. They believe that whoever laughs, lasts. They approach crises with a little levity, which tends to calm the emotions and helps those involved to find new and creative solutions for academic problems. Fun frees the mind. Humor—never leave home without it.

Create a Golden Parachute

First and foremost, upon accepting the job of chair, you should negotiate a sabbatical between terms or at the end of the term to regain currency in your discipline. The most significant and most overlooked responsibility chairs have is to their own personal growth and career development. This critical source of motivation typically is left to the inertia of the past faculty role, the happenstance of the present chair role, or the whim of an unknown future role. To assess your next move from chair, delve into your past, assess the present, and plan for the future. Remember, on the average, chairs serve six years in their administrative posts, with 65 percent returning to faculty status and only one in five continuing in the administrative career path. Ask yourself the following questions:

1. What previous positions have you held in higher education or elsewhere?

2. In what positions were you most productive? Why?

3. What jobs/roles did you do least well? Why?

4. What jobs did you enjoy the most? Why?

5. Which jobs did you enjoy least? Why?

The past helps shape the future. You need to gain a perspective on the past in order to know what you may wish to pursue in the future. What price have you paid for academic leadership (Gmelch 1992)? The answers to these questions will provide you with that perspective.

HAVE YOU LEFT A LEGACY?

Whether you return to faculty status or move on to academic administration, your term as chair will end. As William Jennings Bryan once commented, "Destiny is not a matter of chance, it is a matter of choice; it is not a thing to be waited for, it is a thing to be achieved." How will you want to be remembered by your colleagues? Did you make a difference? Did you leave a legacy?

We asked hundreds of department chairs to reflect on this question, and they responded in enlightened ways. Some hoped they would be known for their role in faculty development: recruiting competent faculty, promoting women and minorities, and nurturing young faculty members. They wanted to be noted for improving the sense of collegiality, where conflicts were healed, morale was enhanced, and peace was brought to the department. Others wanted to be known for their vision in building a national program, enhancing the department's reputation, and leading the department into the twenty-first century. Some chairs saw their legacy in the manager role, in their maintenance of their programs under rough seas: "The ship is still afloat" and "I kept a leaking lifeboat afloat without throwing anyone to the sharks." Simply stated, they "held down the fort," "kept the place from falling apart," and "kept the program going in times of major financial crisis." Finally, chairs hoped that they would be respected for their personal qualities: honesty, openness, fairness, justice, and altruism. Obviously, these legacies reflect three of the department chair roles; curiously, recognition of their scholarship went unmentioned by any of the chairs.

What is the legacy you would like to leave your department? Heads of departments reflected on their legacy by simply stating they wanted to (1) develop programs, (2) develop people, and (3) do it with decency! Remember, a legacy is built on sustained dedication, strong commitment, and clear purpose. Are you willing to serve long enough to transcend the managerial role and develop strong leadership for your department? One chief executive officer commented, "No executive who begins [a] journey and gives up after three years will ever live to tell a positive story."

Developing the Chair

It is well established that few chairs receive preparation to conceptually understand and professionally balance the duties of their position. The cost of leadership is too great not to invest in the most critical position in the university, the department chair (Green and McDade 1994). Several campuses have designed programs to develop department chairs not as managers but as leaders, in a systematic and continuous manner (Gmelch, Allen, and Melsa 2002). What can we learn from these model campus programs? Are there lessons that can be extrapolated from one campus to another? Several lessons emerged from one such campus model. These should not be viewed as a blueprint. Each campus's unique culture and political and social climates must be taken into consideration when designing campus leadership programs. The seeds sewn on our campus may not grow on others. However, the following lessons learned may help other campuses in search of providing support and balance for their department chairs (see Gmelch, Reason, et al. 2002, 48–51).

- Cohort groups of chairs in leadership development are essential. Chairs do not develop within a vacuum, out of context, and off by themselves. Leadership, by its very nature, is relational, and success depends on the ability to work and interact with others within institutional settings. The quick fix of sending chairs off to weekend seminars has limited sustained learning, institutional understanding, and support for the chairs' balancing acts. Research suggests that the most effective programs include work teams with their supervisors, such that each supports and reinforces each other in skill development and reflective practice.

- Chairs thrive when they have mentors and support networks for guidance and reflection. Leadership is an inner, and often lonely, journey. It is about finding one's voice and the passion to serve. By identifying someone as a support person and confidant, pairing chairs promotes reflective dialogue and combats the "lonely crowd" syndrome. Chairs flourish within a support group and with a trusted colleague acting as a mentor, partner, and/or coach.

- Chair development must entail continuous learning opportunities. As educators, we know that learning that occurs in distributed periods of training is retained longer than learning undertaken in one-time programs. The literature on how one becomes an expert argues that developing leadership requires intensive, focused learning over extended periods of time. To be truly successful, a leadership program for chairs must adopt a systems approach that builds on continual, progressive, and sequential development and constructive feedback. Chairs can only find balance through continuous development and feedback.

- Department chair leadership development requires a supportive culture. Chairs are busy people. For them to take time from their commitment to their duties for professional development opportunities, they need to feel that leadership development opportunities are supported and valued. While simple encouragement has a significant influence, researchers have found that managers who perceive a greater measure of support from their immediate bosses (deans) report a higher degree of motivation to attend and learn from training.

- Professional development programs for chairs must be built around a single, well-defined model of leadership development. One of the biggest problems most leadership development programs must overcome is a vague concept of what they are trying to accomplish. As suggested in the beginning of this chapter, one such model includes the components of contextual understanding of the roles of chairs, the skills chairs need to perform those roles, and the art of reflective practice. Others may be equally valid. Nevertheless, for chairs to find their balance and become productive scholars and leaders, they must understand the nature of their job, the skills needed to provide them with balance, and the ability to reflect and adjust on what really matters in their personal and professional lives.

Developing faculty into department leaders is both a privilege and a responsibility of university administrators and department chairs themselves. Finding balance in leadership is a reciprocal relationship—it requires both the institution's commitment and the faculty's receptivity to the call to leadership. The future of universities and colleges depends on answering the call with commitment and balance.

Nothing can substitute for leadership in times of change and chaos in higher education. The time for amateur administration is over. It is within your capacity to respond to the challenge of the call for department leadership. We hope this book has helped you to reflect on your responsibility as a leader, manager, faculty developer, and scholar. Seize the moment!

BIBLIOGRAPHY

Acker, D.G., ed. 1999. *Leadership for higher education in agriculture: Proceedings of the Global Consortium, Amsterdam, Netherlands.* Ames: Iowa State University.

Aldag, R.J., and B. Joseph. 2000. *Leadership and vision.* New York: Lebhar-Friedman Books.

Amit, R., C. Lucier, M.A. Hitt, and R.D. Nixon. 2002. Strategies for creating value in the entrepreneurial millennium. In *Creating value: Winners in the new business environment,* ed. M.A. Hitt, R. Amit, C. Lucier, and R.D. Nixon, 1–12. Oxford, UK: Blackwell.

Andersen, D.A. 2002. The deans of the future. In *The deans' balancing acts: Education leaders and the challenges they face,* ed. W.H. Gmelch. Washington, D.C.: AACTE Publications.

Astin, A.W., and H.S. Astin. 2000. *Leadership reconsidered: Engaging higher education in social change.* Battle Creek, Mich.: Kellogg Foundation.

Barney, J.B., and A.M. Arikan. 2001. The resource-based view: Origins and implications. In *Handbook of strategic management,* ed. M.A. Hitt, R.E. Freeman, and J.R. Harrison, 124–188. Oxford, UK: Blackwell.

Beer, M., and R.A. Eisenstat. 2000. The silent killers of strategy implementation and learning. *MIT Sloan Management Review* 41(4):29–40.

Beineke, J.A., and R.H. Sublett. 1999. *Leadership lessons and competencies: Learning from the Kellogg National Fellowship Program.* Battle Creek, Mich.: Kellogg Foundation.

Berger, A.A. 1993. *Improving writing skills.* Newbury Park, Calif.: Sage.

Birnbaum, R. 1988. Presidential searches and the discovery of organizational goals. *Journal of Higher Education* 59(5):489–509.

———. 1990. *How colleges work: The cybernetics of academic organization and leadership.* San Francisco: Jossey-Bass.

Block, P. 1990. *The empowered manager: Positive political skills at work.* San Francisco: Jossey-Bass.

Boice, R. 1992. *The new faculty member.* San Francisco: Jossey-Bass.

Bowman, R.F., Jr. 2002. The real work of department chair. *The Clearing House* 75(3):158–162.

Boyer, E.L. 1990. *Scholarship reconsidered: Priorities of the professoriate.* San Francisco: Jossey-Bass.

Braskamp, L.A., and J.C. Ory. 1994. *Assessing faculty work: Enhancing individual and institutional performance.* San Francisco: Jossey-Bass.

Bridges, W., and S. Mitchell. 2000. Leading transition: A new model for change. *Leader to Leader* 16:30–36.

Brown, L.M. 2001. Leading leadership development in universities: A personal story. *Journal of Management Inquiry* 10(4):312–325.

Buckingham, M., and C. Coffman. 1999. *First, break all the rules: What the world's greatest managers do differently.* New York: Simon and Schuster.

Burns, J.M. 1978. *Leadership.* New York: Harper and Row.

Cameron, K. 1983. Strategic responses to conditions of decline: Higher education and the private sector. *Journal of Higher Education* 54:359–380.

Carroll, J.B. 1991. Career paths of department chairs. *Research in Higher Education.* 32(6):669–688.

Carroll, J.B., and W.H. Gmelch. 1992. *A factor-analytic investigation of the role types and profiles of higher education department chairs.* San Francisco: American Educational Research Conference. (ERIC Document Reproduction Service No. ED 345 629.)

———. 1994. Department chairs' perceptions of the relative importance of their duties. *Journal for Higher Education Management* 10(1):49–63.

Carroll, J.B., and M. Wolverton. 2004. Who becomes a department chair. In *The Career Cycle of the Department Chair,* ed. W.H. Gmelch and J.S. Schuh. New Directions Sourcebook. San Francisco: Jossey-Bass.

Centra, J.A. 1993. *Reflective faculty evaluation: Enhancing teaching and determining faculty effectiveness.* San Francisco: Jossey-Bass.

Chaffee, E.E. 1983. The role of rationality in university budgeting. *Research in Higher Education* 19:387–406.

Chemers, M.M. 1993. An integrative theory of leadership. In *Leadership theory and Research: Perspectives and directions,* ed. M.M. Chemers and R. Ayman, 293–319. San Diego, Calif.: Academic Press.

Collins, J., and J. Porras. 1997. *Built to last: Successful habits of visionary companies.* New York: HarperBusiness.

Conger, J.A. 1992. *Learning to lead: The art of transforming managers into leaders.* San Francisco: Jossey-Bass.

Conger, J.A., and B. Benjamin. 1999. *Building leaders: How successful companies develop the next generation.* San Francisco: Jossey-Bass.

Creighton, L. 2001. Mission almost impossible. *ASEE Prism* 11(1):40–42.

Creswell, J.W., D.W. Wheeler, A.T. Seagren, N.J. Egly, and K.D. Beyer. 1990. *The academic chairperson's handbook.* Lincoln: University of Nebraska Press.

Davidson, C.I., and S.A. Ambrose. 1994. *The new professor's handbook.* Bolton, Mass.: Anker.

Dooris, M.J. 2002–2003. Two decades of strategic planning. *Planning Higher Education* 31(2):26–32.

Drucker, P.F. 1974. *Management: Tasks, responsibilities, practice.* New York: Harper and Row.

Eble, K.E. 1978. *The art of administration.* San Francisco: Jossey-Bass.

Eckel, P., M. Green, and B. Hill. 2001. *Riding the waves of change: Insights from transforming institutions.* Washington, D.C.: American Council on Education.

Ericsson, K.A., and J. Smith. 1991. *Towards a general theory of expertise.* Cambridge, UK: Cambridge University Press.

Bibliography

Ericsson, K.A., R.T. Krampe, and C. Tesch-Romer. 1993. The role of deliberate practices in the acquisition of expert performance. *Psychological Review* 100(3):363–406.

Fisher, R., and W. Ury. 1991. *Getting to yes: Negotiating agreement without giving in.* New York: Penguin Books.

Gardner, J.W. 1990. *On leadership.* New York: Free Press.

Gibson, G.W. 1992. *Good start: A guidebook for new faculty in liberal arts colleges.* Bolton, Mass.: Anker.

Glassick, C.E., M.T. Huber, and G.I. Maeroff. 1997. *Scholarship assessed: Evaluation of the professoriate.* San Francisco: Jossey-Bass.

Gmelch, W.H. 1983. Stress for success: How to optimize your performance. *Theory into Practice* 22(1):7–15.

———. 1987. What colleges and universities can do about faculty stress. In *Coping with stress,* ed. P. Seldin, 23–31. New York: Jossey-Bass.

———. 1992. Paying the price for academic leadership: Department chair tradeoffs. *Educational Record* 72(3):45–49.

———. 1993. *Coping with faculty stress.* Newbury Park, Calif.: Sage.

———. 1994. The paradox of the swivel chair. *Journal of Leadership Studies* 1(2):126–130.

———. 1995. The department chair's role in improving teaching. In *Improving college teaching,* ed. P. Seldin, 137–149. Bolton, Mass.: Anker.

———. 1996a. Department chairs under siege: Resolving the web of conflict. In *Conflict management in higher education,* ed. S. Holton, 35–42. San Francisco: Jossey-Bass.

———. 1996b. It's about time. *Academe* 83(5):22–27.

———. 1998. The Janus syndrome: Managing conflict from the middle. In *Mending the cracks in the ivory tower,* ed. S.A. Holton, 28–45. Bolton, Mass.: Anker.

———. 2001. Building leadership capacity for university transformation. Paper presented at the International Conference for Improving University Learning and Teaching, June, Johannesburg, South Africa.

———. 2003. Transitions of leadership: From a department chair to a dean. In *Bridging the gap: Leadership, technology, and organizational change for deans and department chairs,* ed. M. Johnson, D. Hanna, and D. Olcott, Jr. Madison, Wisc.: Atwood.

———. 2004. The department chairs' balancing act. In *The career cycle of the department chair,* ed. W.H. Gmelch and J.S. Schuh. New Directions Sourcebook. San Francisco: Jossey-Bass.

———, ed. 2002. *Deans' balancing acts: Education leaders and the challenges they face.* Washington, D.C.: American Association of Colleges for Teacher Education Publications.

Gmelch, W.H., B. Allen, and J. Melsa. 2002. Building a campus model for leadership development. *The Department Chair* 13(2):13–15.

Gmelch, W.H., and J.B. Burns. 1993. The cost of academic leadership: Department chair stress. *Innovative Higher Education* 17(4):259–270.

———. 1994. Sources of stress for academic department chairpersons. *Journal of Educational Administration* 32(1):79–94.

Gmelch, W.H., J.B. Burns, J.B. Carroll, S. Harris, and D. Wentz. 1992. *Center for the Study of the Department Chair: 1992 survey.* Pullman: Washington State University.

Gmelch, W.H., J.B. Carroll, R.G. Seedorf, and D. Wentz. 1990. *Center for the Study of the Department Chair: 1990 survey.* Pullman: Washington State University.

Gmelch, W.H., and W. Chan. 1994. *Thriving on stress for success.* Newbury Park, Calif.: Corwin Press.

Gmelch, W.H., and N.S. Glasman. 1976. Purposes of evaluation of university instructors: Definitions, delineations, and dimensions. *Canadian Journal of Higher Education* 6(2):37–55.

Gmelch, W.H., and B. Houchen. 1994. The balancing act of community college chairs. *Academic Leadership* 2:4–11.

Gmelch, W.H., N.P. Lovrich, and P.K. Wilke. 1984. Stress in academe: A national perspective. *Research in Higher Education* 20(4):477–490.

Gmelch, W.H., and V.D. Miskin. 1993. *Leadership skills for department chairs.* Bolton, Mass.: Anker.

Gmelch, W.H., and F.W. Parkay. 1999. Becoming a department chair: Negotiating the transition from scholar to administrator. Paper presented at the American Educational Research Association, April, Montreal, Canada.

Gmelch, W.H., R.D. Reason, J.S. Schuh, and M.D. Shelley. 2002. *The call for academic leaders: The academic leadership forum report.* Ames: Iowa State University.

Gmelch, W.H., and J. Sarros. 1996. How to work with your dean: Voices of American and Australian department chairs. *The Department Chair* 6(4):1–19.

Gmelch, W.H., J. Sarros, M. Wolverton, and M.L. Wolverton. 1998. *Australian national study of academic deans.* Pullman, Wash.: Center for Academic Leadership.

Gmelch, W.H., and R.G. Seedorf. 1989. Academic leadership under siege: The ambiguity and imbalance of department chairs. *Journal for Higher Education Management* 5(1):37–44.

Gmelch, W.H., P.K. Wilke, and N.P. Lovrich. 1986. Dimensions of stress among university faculty: Factor analytic results from national study. *Research in Higher Education* 24(3):266–286.

Gmelch, W.H., M. Wolverton, M.L. Wolverton, and M. Hermanson. 1996. *National study of academic deans in higher education.* Pullman, Wash.: Center for Academic Leadership.

Gonyea, M.A. 1980. Determining academic staff needs, allocation, and utilization. In *A handbook of planning and institutional research,* ed. P. Jedamus, M.W. Peterson, and Associates, 364–372. San Francisco: Jossey-Bass.

Gorham, D., W.H. Gmelch, W. Parkman, and E. Rose. 2002. The engineering deans' summit on technological literacy. Paper presented at the Annual Meeting of the American Association of Colleges of Teacher Education, New York.

Gordon, J. 2002. Using business strategy to drive leadership development. *Employment Relations Today* 28(4):61–67.

Green, M.F., and S.A. McDade. 1994. *Investing in higher education: A handbook of leadership development.* Phoenix, Ariz.: Oryx Press.

Grobmyer, J.E. 2002. Putting your financially based strategic plan into action. *Trustee* 55(1):30–33.

Hackman, J.D. 1985. Power and centrality in the allocation of resources in colleges and universities. *Administrative Science Quarterly* 30:61–77.

Harris-Sledge, S.E. 1994. *Work orientations and work realities of department chairpersons: A qualitative study.* Ph.D. dissertation, Washington State University.

Hecht, I., M. Higgerson, W.H. Gmelch, and A. Tucker. 1999. *The department chair as academic leader.* Phoenix, Ariz.: ACE/Oryx Press.

Hickson, M., and D.W. Stacks, eds. 1992. *Effective communication for academic chairs.* Albany: State University of New York Press.

Bibliography

Higgerson, M.L. 1996. *Communication skills for department chairs*. Bolton, Mass.: Anker.

Hitt, M.A., and R.D. Ireland. 2002. The essence of strategic leadership: Managing human and social capital. *Journal of Leadership and Organizational Studies* 9(1):3–15.

Hogan, C. 1992. Strategies for enhancing empowerment. *Training and Management Development Methods* 6(3):25–39.

Houchen, B.C., and W.H. Gmelch. 1994. *Center for the Study of the Department Chair: Community college survey*. Pullman: Washington State University.

Huffman, J. 2003. The role of shared values and vision in creating professional learning communities. *NASSP Bulletin* 87(637):21–34.

Hynes, W.J. 1990. Successful proactive recruiting strategies: Quest for the best. In *Enhancing departmental leadership: The roles of the chairperson*, ed. J. Bennett, and D. Figuli, 51–61. New York: American Council on Education/Macmillan.

Jackson, J.F.L. 2002. Executive behavior patterns of deans. In *The dean's balancing acts: Education leaders and the challenges they face*, ed. W.H. Gmelch, pp. 89–98. Washington, D.C.: AACTE Publications.

Johnson, D.W., R.T. Johnson, and K. Smith. 1998. *Active learning: Cooperation in the college classroom*. Edina, Minn.: Interaction Book.

Kable, J. 1992. The budget process. In *Effective communication for academic chairs*, ed. M. Hickson and D.W. Stacks, 81–89. Albany: State University of New York Press.

Klein, G. 1998. *The sources of power: How people make decisions*. Cambridge, Mass.: MIT Press.

Kotter, J.P. 1990. What leaders really do. *Harvard Business Review*, May-June, pp. 3–11.

Kouzes, J.M., and B.Z. Posner. 2003. *Exemplary leadership*. San Francisco: Jossey-Bass.

Layzell,, D.T. 1996. Faculty workload and productivity: Recurrent issues and new imperatives. *Review of Higher Education* 19:267–281.

Leaming, D.R. 1998. *Academic leadership*. Bolton, Mass.: Anker.

Likert, R. 1961. *New patterns of management*. New York: McGraw-Hill.

Lovett, C.M. 1993. Listening to the faculty grapevine. *AAHE Bulletin* 43(3):3–5.

Lucas, A.F. 1994. *Strengthening departmental leadership*. San Francisco: Jossey-Bass.

———. 2000. *Leading academic change: Essential roles for department chairs*. San Francisco: Jossey-Bass.

Mabry, R.H. 1993. Giving faculty their own budgets for research and teaching. Paper presented at the Tenth Annual Conference on Academic Chairpersons: Selecting, Motivating, Evaluating and Rewarding Faculty.

Makadok, R. 2001. Toward a synthesis of the resource-based and dynamic-capability view of rent creation..*Strategic Management Journal* 22:387–401.

Marchese, T.J., and J.F. Lawrence. 1989. *The search committee handbook: A guide to recruiting administrators*. Washington, D.C.: American Association for Higher Education.

McKeachie, W.J. 1999. *Teaching tips: A guidebook for the beginning college teacher*. 10th ed. Lexington, Mass.: D.C. Heath.

McLaughlin, G.W., J.R. Montgomery, and L.F. Malpass. 1975. Selected characteristics, roles, goals, and satisfactions of department chairmen in state and land-grant institutions. *Research in Higher Education* 3:243–259.

Mintzberg, H. 1973. *The nature of managerial work*. New York: Harper and Row.

Miskin, V.D., and W.H. Gmelch. 1985. Quality leadership for quality teams. *Training and Development Journal* 39(5):122–180.

Moses, I., and E. Roe. 1990. *Heads and chairs: Managing academic departments.* Queensland, Australia: University of Queensland Press.

Murray, J.P. 1993. Hiring: Back to the basics. *The Department Chair* 3(4):16–17.

O'Reilly, B. 1994. What's killing the business school deans of America. *Fortune,* August 8:64–68.

Orwig, M.D., and J.K. Caruthers. 1980. Improving academic management. In *A handbook of planning and institutional research,* ed. P. Jedamus, M.W. Peterson, and Associates, 341–363. San Francisco: Jossey-Bass.

Pines, M. 1980. Psychological hardiness. *Psychology Today,* December.

Polglase, K.J. 2003. Leadership is everyone's business. *Leadership* 32(5):24–27.

Priem, R.L., and J.E. Butler. 2001. Is the resource-based view a useful perspective for strategic research? *Academy of Management Review* 26:22–40.

Purser, R.E., and S. Cabana. 1997. Involve employees at every level of strategic planning. *Quality Progress* 30(5):66–71.

Randolph, A., and B.Z. Posner. 1988. *Effective project planning and management: Getting the job done.* Englewood Cliffs, N.J.: Prentice-Hall.

Ready, D. 1994. *Champions of change,* 26–28. Lexington, Mass.: International Consortium for Executive Development Research.

Rosse, J.G., and R.A. Levin. 2003. *Academic administrator's guide to hiring.* San Francisco: Jossey-Bass.

Rosser, V.J., L.K. Johnsrud, and R.H. Heck. 2003. Academic deans and directors: Assessing their effectiveness from individual and institutional perspectives. *Journal of Higher Education* 74(1):1–25.

Rost, J.C. 1993. *Leadership for the twenty-first century.* Westport, Conn.: Praeger.

Rubin, I. 1980. Retrenchment and flexibility in public organizations. In *Fiscal stress and public policy,* ed. C.H. Levin and I. Rubin. Beverly Hills, Calif.: Sage.

Sarros, J.C., W.H. Gmelch, and G.A. Tanewski. 1997. The role of department head in Australian universities: Tasks and stresses. *Higher Education Research and Development* 16(1):9–24.

———. 1998. Role stress and satisfaction of academic department heads. *International Journal of Business Studies* 6(1):97–123.

Schick, A.G. 1985. University budgeting: Administrative perspective and process. *Academy of Management Review* 10:794–802.

Schmidtlein, F.A. 1990. Why linking budgets to plan has proved difficult in higher education. *Planning for Higher Education* 18(2):9–23.

Schon, D.A. 1983. *The reflective practitioner: How professionals think in action.* New York: Basic Books.

Seagren, A.T., J.W. Creswell, and D.W. Wheeler. 1993. *The department chair: New roles, responsibilities, and challenges.* Higher Education Report One. Washington, D.C.: ASHE-ERIC.

Seagren, A.T., D.W. Wheeler, J.W. Creswell, M.T. Miller, and K. VanHorn-Grassmeyer. 1994. *Academic leadership in community colleges.* Lincoln: University of Nebraska Press.

Seedorf, R.G. 1989. *The academic department chair: A descriptive study.* Document #1002. Pullman: Center for the Study of the Department Chair, Washington State University.

———. 1990. *Transition to leadership: The university department chair.* Pullman: Center for the Study of the Department Chair, Washington State University.

Seldin, P. 1994. *Changing practices in faculty evaluation.* San Francisco: Jossey-Bass.

Bibliography

————. 1997. *The teaching portfolio: A practical guide to improved performance and promotion/ tenure decisions.* Bolton, Mass.: Anker.

Seldin, P., and Associates. 1995. *Improving college teaching.* Bolton, Mass.: Anker.

Seldin, P., and M.L. Higgerson. 2002. *The administrative portfolio.* Bolton, Mass.: Anker.

Sessa, V.I., and J.J. Taylor. 2000. *Executive selection: Strategies for success.* San Francisco: Jossey-Bass.

Smart, J., and J. Elton. 1976. Duties performed by department chairmen in Holland's model environments. *Journal of Educational Psychology* 68(2):194–204.

Smelser, N.J. 1993. *Effective committee service.* Newbury Park, Calif.: Sage.

Sparks, D. 1999. Real-life view: Here's what a true learning community looks like. *Journal of Staff Development* 20(4):53–57.

Taylor, E.P., and G.E. Kundy. 1991. Faculty perceptions of the budget process. *The Department Chair Newsletter* 2(2):8.

Thomas, J., and J.S. Schuh. 2004. Socializing department chairs. In *The career cycle of the department chair,* ed. W.H. Gmelch and J.S. Schuh. San Francisco: Jossey-Bass.

Thomas, M.D., and W.L. Bainbridge. 2002. Sharing the glory. *Leadership* 31(3):12–15.

Thompson, A.A., Jr., and A.J. Strickland, III. 1998. *Crafting and implementing strategy: Text and readings.* Boston: Irwin/McGraw-Hill.

Thyer, B.A. 1994. *Successful publishing in scholarly journals.* Newbury Park, Calif.: Sage.

Tucker, A. 1992. *Chairing the academic department: Leadership among peers.* 2nd ed.. New York: American Council on Education/Oryx.

Tucker, A., and R.A. Bryan. 1988. *The academic dean: Dove, dragon, and diplomat.* New York: American Council on Education and Macmillan.

Ury, W. 1993. *Getting past no: Negotiating with difficult people.* New York: Bantam Books.

Vandament, W.E. 1989. *Managing money in higher education.* San Francisco: Jossey-Bass.

VanderWaerdt, L. 1982. *Affirmative action in higher education.* New York: Garland.

Volk, C.S., S. Slaughter, and S.L. Thomas. 2001. Models of Institutional Resource Allocation. *Journal of Higher Education* 72(4):387–413.

Waggaman, J.S. 1991. *Strategies and consequences: Managing the costs in higher education.* Higher Education Report No. 8. Washington D.C.: ASHE-ERIC.

Weimer, M. 1993. *Improving your classroom teaching.* Newbury Park, Calif.: Sage.

Wergin, J.F. 2003. *Departments that work: Building and sustaining cultures of excellence in academic programs.* Bolton, Mass.: Anker.

Whicker, M.L., J.J. Kronenfeld, and R.A. Strickland. 1993. *Getting tenure.* Newbury Park, Calif.: Sage.

Wilke, P.K., W.H. Gmelch, and N.P. Lovrich. 1985. Stress and productivity: Evidence of the inverted U-function. *Public Productivity Review* 9(4):342–356.

Wolverton, M., and W.H. Gmelch. 2002. *The college dean: Leading from within.* Phoenix, Ariz.: ACE/Oryx Press, Greenwood Press.

Wolverton, M., W.H. Gmelch, and D. Sorenson. 1998. The department as double agent: The call for department change and renewal. *Innovative Higher Education* 22(3):203–216.

Wolverton, M., W.H. Gmelch, M.L. Wolverton, and J. Sarros. 1999. A comparison of department chair tasks in Australia and the United States. *Higher Education* 38:333–350.

Yukl, G.A. 1994. *Leadership in organizations.* Englewood Cliffs, N.J.: Prentice-Hall.

INDEX

About the Authors

Walter H. Gmelch will be Dean of the School of Education at the University of San Francisco in August 2004. He is currently Dean of the College of Education at Iowa State University and formerly served in the roles of Dean, Associate Dean, Department Chair and Professor at Washington State University. Gmelch also directs the National Center for Academic Leadership at Iowa State University. He earned a Ph.D. in the Educational Executive Program from the University of California (Santa Barbara), a masters in Business Administration from the University of California (Berkeley), and a bachelors degree from Stanford University.

As educator, management consultant, university administrator, and former business executive, Gmelch has conducted research and written extensively on the topics of leadership, team development, conflict, and stress and time management. He has published over 100 articles, 20 books, and 200 scholarly papers in national and international journals. Gmelch has authored books on department leadership with Val Miskin and others (*Chairing an Academic Department, Leadership Skills for Department Chairs, The Department Chair as Academic Leader, and Productivity Teams: Beyond Quality Circles*), college leadership (*The Changing Nature of the Academic Dean, Deans' Balancing Acts*, and *College Deans: Leading from Within*), and stress management (*Coping with Faculty Stress* and *Beyond Stress to Effective Management*).

Today Gmelch is one of the leading researchers in the study of academic leaders in higher education, serving as editor of two journals and on the editorial board of a half dozen other journals including *The Department Chair, Innovative Higher Education, Academic Leadership,* and the *Center for Academic Leadership Newsletter*. During the 1990s he directed two national studies of 1,600 university department chairs in the United States, one study of 1,580 Australian department heads, another investigation of

1,000 community college chairs, and recently has completed an international study of 2,000 academic deans in Australia and America.

Gmelch has received numerous honors including a Kellogg National Fellowship, the University Council for Educational Administration Distinguished Professor Award, the Faculty Excellence Award for Research, and the Education Press Award of America. In addition, he served on the Danforth Leadership Program and as an Australian Research Fellow.

Val D. Miskin is Director of Graduate Programs in the College of Business at Washington State University. He received his Ph.D. in administration from Washington State University, an M.B.A. from Utah State University, and a bachelor's degree in psychology from Brigham Young University. A one time business owner, he has more than 15 years of corporate managerial experience in management training and leadership development. He has presented papers at the national meetings of the Academy of Management, the National Conference of Entrepreneurial Studies, and the National Chairpersons Conference. His work has appeared in the *American Society for Training and Development Journal, Personnel, Frontiers of Entrepreneurship Research, the Journal of Staff, Program, and Organization Development*, and the *Journal of Small Business Strategy*. He is coauthor of *Productivity Teams: Beyond Quality Circles, Productivity and Team Building: How Groups Become Teams,* and *Leadership Skills for Department Chairs.* He currently teaches in the areas of strategic leadership and human resource management. He has conducted hundreds of leadership seminars and strategic management workshops over the years, and he regularly provides consulting services to both business and nonprofit organizations.